Heroes Publi

ROTATION,
ROTATION, ROTATION
a season at Anfield

Steven Kelly

First published in Great Britain in 2008 by
Heroes Publishing.
P.O. Box 1703, Perry Barr,
Birmingham B42 1UZ.

–
ISBN 9780955970818

Cover design: www.nineteen76-designs.co.uk

Printed by Thomson Litho

Acknowledgements

Thanks to:

Tony Leen and Colm O'Connor at the *Irish Examiner* for giving me the gig, and to Allan Prosser for help and advice ever since.

Bernard, Richard, Trizia and Martyn for setting the standard and keeping me on my toes.

All the writers and cartoonists who helped me with the fanzine for so long. Barry, Billy, Chris, Ian, Mark, Neil and Tony who stood in all weathers for 19 years helping me sell the damn thing.

Gary, Karl, Paul and Laura for their invaluable work on the website www.ttwar.net (check out www.lfconline.com too) and Dave for making the book happen.

Mum, Dad, Kathy and San – the best family on the planet. John and May Harrison, for having such a wonderful daughter. Janet, who complains so little and means so much, to whom this book is lovingly dedicated.

Contents

Preface

These columns are reproduced with the kind permission of the *Irish Examiner*. In all cases they are the originals, the paper having amended a few of them for publication, so if any sensitive souls are aggrieved they should direct all correspondence to me.

They appeared every Wednesday, which is why you'll notice some nonplussed references to the Champions League games that took place just after my Monday afternoon deadline. It also explains why so very little of the actual football is mentioned, given that everyone knew full well what had happened by then. I'm sure there are other tomes which will inform you as to who passed to whom, whose shot deflected off whatever part of the opponent's body and which stupid Norwegian git headed through his own net and almost single-handedly wrecked our chances of a third final in four years.

Not that I'm bitter.

Introduction

For far too long Liverpool has been a football club at war with itself. It is usually only a matter of time before the latest uneasy truce is shattered by a public outburst, usually from one of its new owners, usually the loudmouth Hicks. Fans have marched, chanted and formed pressure groups, ever mindful of protests inside the ground that divide us and take attention away from what is or ought to be the real focal point – the team. Even the Americans can't stand each other now, and all reports of renewed unity must be taken with a pinch of salt. The club's previous administrators allegedly plot behind the scenes in order to undo the enormous damage caused by their own naivety/incompetence/greed (delete any if you like, but all three can be persuasively argued). In the background waits, somewhat impatiently, the financial wing of the United Arab Emirates, hoping there will still be something left to salvage. The media, meanwhile, frolic delightedly in the rubble, their usual pernicious creativity unnecessary for once as the reporting of each new eruption of ineptitude virtually writes itself.

So all hope is lost, no? You'd be surprised. In the face of such chaos the manager and his players have somehow managed to close the gap on United by eight points since 2006-07, a season that had its numerous cracks papered over by another Champions League final. Those last few words sound terribly flippant I know, but only a Riise brainstorm kept us out of the final this time around. The league saw an additional eight points thanks largely to not taking a breather in the final stretch, as we did in 2007. The arrival of the long awaited 20-goal striker didn't hurt either, especially as he edged his way past the 30 mark. Sadly there was never a time when Liverpool fans looked at the table and thought, "This could be our season." Not after the turn of the year, anyway.

It all began so well, too. After the six-goal thrashing of Derby County a friend told me I had a huge grin on my face. He walked straight into a lamppost as a result. Needless to say such rampant giddiness could never last. By autumn the usual grumbles about Rotation grew louder, the flames fanned by a mischievous press smelling the blood of another managerial casualty. Which would then be their cue to put the boot into an impatient club and its shallow fans! It's called a win-win situation.

It was Rafa's fourth season, he had spent a fair chunk of money on new players and it was seen as the time to deliver. Fair enough, really. And for a short while it looked as though he actually might do it. Enter Laurel & Hardy. Now the owners were the story and all hell had broken loose. Liverpudlian protocol dictates that everything is Hicks' fault. Admittedly you do wonder how the man ties his own shoelaces, never mind amassed a fortune but it was all a tad too convenient, especially for the manager. Criticism of his methods had begun to grow, but a few wins and the Klinsmann rumour helped to construct a pedestal from which it would take a nuclear blast to shift him.

Somewhat bizarrely it was now cast in stone that Rafa's quest had been insufficiently funded. Roman Abramovich continues to cast his shadow. In the modern era Wenger and especially Ferguson's initial successes were not earned by outspending their rivals, but there was no point arguing any more. Fed on scraps and heckled from across the Atlantic, it was a miracle Benitez kept us going at all. Or that's where the party line tows you.

Maybe we can be a bit too cynical sometimes because Liverpool are undoubtedly better than they were a year ago and optimism might not be such a bewildering concept after all.

True, its continuance will certainly depend on resolving problems off the field and new acquisitions on it. This is a team that is more than a match for anybody when everything slots into place and we get the breaks, but it can also be destabilised in a way that United's cannot.

Despite a nation-wide belief that Benitez is the only manager who changes his team around, Ferguson is also capable of shuffling his pack with less than successful results (Bolton and Chelsea away to name but two) but it is rarely anything more than a blip. Rafa rested both Gerrard and Torres at Portsmouth after a week largely spent moaning about internationals. Though a 0-0 wasn't the worst result in the world it began almost two months of draws which cancelled out the occasional lucky win. When he later treated Reading with a certain disdain another eight weeks of mediocrity ensued – and with such minutiae the title is gone for another year. The majority of fans did not hold it against him, preferring instead to believe that a hierarchical choice between beating Marseille or packing his bags had forced the manager's hand against a side that was ultimately relegated. It's a questionable theory in truth, but as things began to slowly unravel the connivance of the Americans and revelations of their subterfuge with Jurgen Klinsmann became such a massive stumbling block in the collective Red psyche that it was felt no manager could possibly have overcome it.

Odd though that when Gillett and Hicks publicly went for each other's throats during the spring, with the latter also attempting to take out Rick Parry for good measure, Liverpool's form wasn't affected in any way. The football was better, Gerrard and Torres were ideally suited to a new formation even though it sidelined and ultimately forced out Peter Crouch. The political bickering went on and on, getting nastier if such a thing was possible, and yet the team, in sharp contrast to December and January, remained in full control of its destiny. It might seem to those of an excessively cynical nature as though off-the-pitch problems became a distraction only when it was expedient for the manager to think so, or when his own position was under threat.

What we have always had in the Benitez era is feast or famine. Istanbul was a colossal achievement, yet the league performance was so weak even Everton overtook us. In 2005-06 there were four significant sequences of league results; two saw relegation form while two saw perfect winning records. The year after saw only one such oasis, to go with the ultimately calamitous trip to Athens, while we certainly had United and co in our sights at Christmas this time around. The incredible finish saw us drop only nine points out of a possible 45, yet it did not go unnoticed that seven of those were lost away to the other 'Big Four' sides and such a great run of form hardly put a dent in United's February lead. Chilling, to put it mildly, and such highs and lows do mean there is a touch of schizophrenia within the support.

The optimists will point to the inauspicious face-offs with United in particular and claim that's the only obstruction to our rightful place at the summit, something we also tried on Chelsea fans in 2006. Well it's a theory anyway. There is, however, reluctance or an inability to finish other more lowly opponents off, leaving you in dread of the late equaliser that can ruin a whole afternoon's grind. There were far too many drawn games. This ruthlessness is absolutely essential if we're to challenge in any meaningful way. The pessimists will say we've waited four years for it, what difference is another one going to make? That's what 'faith' is for I suppose. The final months saw Rafa stick with a formation that produced goals, wins and good football. The opponents were often weak as water but the same teams weren't being swatted aside in the first half of the season so there was definitely a change for the better. A lot of us are happy enough with the players and the manager does deserve enormous credit for assembling this squad. There is still a fear that the biggest change has to take place within Rafa's own head. That's if he is sticking around of course, it's been at least six months since he was last linked to the Real Madrid job and he's surely due another flounce soon.

Though talk of a title challenge had become risible by late January, only the churlish could deny that we produced an outstanding finish thanks in no small part to a rejuvenated Gerrard and the deadly finishing of the Kop's latest hero. Fernando Torres has been a revelation, if you can say such a thing about a £20-million investment. Supporters have analysed the statistics and come up with various schemes in order to get the team back on top, such as the aforementioned beating of Manchester United, instead of cowering in a corner and asking not to be hurt as we tend to do under Benitez. A reduction in the manager's occasionally bewildering overuse of his squad is another, though it's not quite as random as the malignant media would have you believe. The main idea that took hold of too many supporters' minds in the last few years has been "Give Rafa what he wants"; in a word, Money.

It has become an incontrovertible truth nowadays that you cannot challenge for the title without spending as much as Chelsea or United. Since we are trailing them in the table on a regular basis some want us to spend more than they do to bridge that gap. It has been a saddening display of naivety and greed. Next year we will no doubt celebrate the 50th anniversary of the arrival of Bill Shankly, the catalyst for so much that followed, yet some of our support has lost touch with how that period of plenty came to be acquired. Success has been woven into the red fabric of the club, a right rather than a privilege, but the fact remains that if you have a great man at the helm you will achieve great things. Luck is important too of course, though not quite in the excessive quantities that our blue brethren constantly assert. Money, enormous great wedges of it, has elbowed its way tackily and brashly to the top of the wants list.

We were even making banners about it, for Christ's sake. Remember when we joked about Joey Jones eating frogs' legs? The casual xenophobia of the 70's makes you wince a little.

Remember when we declared Manchester a trophy-free zone? Hilarious at the time, it makes you cringe now but that's as nothing compared to the current trend. One parodied the Barclays commercial. "Rafa Benitez – priceless/For everything else there's George and Tom." Oh dear! Even that isn't as toe curling as the flag begging (there's no other word for it) the Arabs to come and rescue us. The supporters, once totally preoccupied with the stars on the pitch, were now utterly convinced that money was all that separated us from the ultimate glory.

That's where Hicks and Gillett come in, or at least they were supposed to. Pathetic stunts with bank notes certainly led people to think there would be some kind of personal outlay, but we should all have known full well that there is no such thing as a free lunch. And what if the only cash they could give the manager is the profit from the previous year's success and the sale of players he doesn't want any more? Isn't that the way it's supposed to work? Many have quoted Shankly's 'holy trinity' speech and repeated his belief that directors are only there to sign cheques, a rather simplistic notion if I may blaspheme against the Gospel According To Bill for just a second. It blithely ignores the fact that Shankly was an all-time Great who dragged the club from the depths of despair to the top of the English game in four-and-a-half years. He had probably earned the right to have his judgement backed, while Benitez is still finishing in fourth place albeit a lot closer than Houllier managed in 2004. Even if we do accept Rafa as being cut from the same cloth as Shankly and Paisley they still didn't get their own way all the time and had to show an awful lot of ingenuity.

Much has been made of the investment in the fabulous Torres; you get what you pay for, et cetera. Let's take that forward position as the focus for our research into what made Liverpool not only great but also dominant between 1970 and 1990. We bring in Keegan, turn him into a superstar and sell him for a huge profit. We use that money to buy Dalglish. We pull the same trick with Ian Rush and use his fee to buy Beardsley and Aldridge, with enough left over for John Barnes. Open any book about the Reds, count up the goals, the trophies and the magic those players brought us for a grand total payment of NOTHING. Then look through the 'modern' era; Saunders, Clough, Collymore, Heskey, Diouf, Cisse and Kuyt combined can't even get close to the goal tally of the discoveries Owen or Fowler in the same period. We're all mightily relieved that Fernando has done so well but he's the exception to the current red rule. If you want to know how Liverpool FC lost its way it's an interesting microcosm of our ills and one that can be applied to other positions. Hansen versus Babb, anyone?

So does Rafa have this ingenuity? There are hopes for the likes of Skrtel and Agger, but even that doesn't match up to their predecessors Hyypia, Henchoz and the great Jamie Carragher. Rafa's record with strikers certainly wasn't too impressive before his cherubic compatriot arrived on the scene. It seems much easier for fans to point at the likes of Torres and Mascherano, then claim this is the way it has to be done and that foresight is a thing of the past. It isn't obviously, but over the last year or so I've found myself head-banging a brick wall trying to convince people that we're not managed by the second coming of Christ (with goatee). The columns reflect this only too well, but you'll get to those in due course.

They appear every Wednesday during the season in the *Irish Examiner*. I came to get the 'job' via my writing for the fanzine *Through The Wind & Rain*, and anyone who knows anything about RTE's extraordinary Premiership and Champions League coverage will know the Irish do love an alternative viewpoint! Distance gives them perspective I suppose, along with freedom from the usual constraints of passion and (occasionally blind) loyalty. It certainly suited me to keep saying what I wanted to say, even if it did not quite tally with the majority's take on matters. Though I've been doing it this way for 19 years (six with the paper) I've never got any better at explaining it!

I couldn't accurately calculate the amount of times I've been asked this question; "How can you call yourself a Liverpool fan?" – but it's been said often, and with feeling. Does it hurt when the Reds lose and does it exhilarate when they win? Yes, on both counts. Will I leap in whenever any individual connected with the club is unfairly maligned? Absolutely, unless it's John Arne Riise. Am I going to simple spew out the party line on any given subject, no matter how ridiculous and hypocritical? No. What would be the point? Liverpool fans gave terrible stick to Chelsea for their plastic achievements and off-the-peg players, but never thought twice when Parry went trawling round the world selling our arses to the highest bidder. There is a difference between the cockneys and us, but it's not so vast that we can be snooty about it.

One of the things that will leap out of these pages is a certain ambivalence towards the manager. Reading back in the light of an excellent conclusion to the season, apart from the unlucky semi-final defeat, some of the comments in January and February seem terribly snide and vindictive I must confess. Rafa's European record, almost three finals in four years, is astonishing but my own take on the Champions League is cynical since the success has tended to overshadow what I feel Liverpool FC ought to be doing, which is making a concerted effort for the Premier League. 18 years is far too long a wait for a club that once dominated this country. There is a fear that the cash prize involved in European advancement has taken the focus, however slightly, off domestic issues and that mere qualification for the Champions League will suffice. Not that any such heresy will ever be uttered in public of course.

The evidence is conflicting to say the least. It's true that Gerrard and Torres were rested at Fratton Park in September, only to start in Portugal three days later. It's also true that an eminently winnable game at Reading saw a bizarre team sheet and even more baffling late substitutions, hardly surprising if pressure was being brought to bear on Benitez to get us through to the knockout stages when a win at Marseille was absolutely vital. However, once we'd secured a last-16 place the Champions League was put on the backburner till February and by the time it resumed against Inter Milan, Liverpool were out of the title race and the FA Cup. Europe could hardly be blamed for that.

I admit I've reached the edge of my patience with the manager and his ability to win us the elusive number 19. Having been here before with Souness, Evans and Houllier it should be easy to take that final step and state categorically (a) he'll never win it and (b) he's got to go – but it's not easier, in fact it's incredibly hard. For one thing there is the measure of the task at hand; to overcome Chelsea with their title credentials and limitless funds, and United with their own war chest and (let us bite the bullet and finally admit it) their all-time great manager. Rafa really would need to be a combination of our own two Giants if he were to pull off such a spectacular coup. With this in mind many fans are fully prepared to be a lot more patient than they have been for previous regimes. Houllier, despite almost losing his life, took us to the brink of such a success in 2002 but within a year had half the support screaming for his head. Patience is a virtue but it's usually none too plentiful in L4.

There is also the irrefutable fact that we clawed our way to a good total despite a year of calamitous intrigue and bitter infighting. I wrote in the winter columns, and still believe, that Rafa played his part in making all of that nonsense worse. There has been some form of revisionism on Internet forums about that bizarre press conference, claiming that he was so out to lunch because he knew the Americans had been talking to Klinsmann. It's possible of course, but the repeated claim he was focussed on coaching his team would surely have been rephrased to include some reference to the German. Having already tested their patience with his "talking, talking" rant after Athens, which ultimately won him the funds for Torres, Babel, Lucas and Benayoun, it did seem like he had gone too far this time.

The supporters sided with the football man, even taking to the streets on his behalf. Some began inflating Rafa's undeniable gifts to an almost Messianic status, yet we've been filling the back pages ever since and often for the wrong reasons. There have been at least four significant sequences of league results since 2004 in which we have seen precisely why Benitez is revered by so many. Now if he can cut out the periods of drought that have also afflicted us in those years we may get somewhere. Sounds easy when you say it like that! It's a little-known fact that, once you've adjusted all our seasons to three points per win over 38 games, Rafa has the third highest points total in our entire history. Which means that Liverpool won 16 of their titles with less than what Benitez achieved in 2006. It does give you some idea of the daunting task we face in overtaking those above us. Recent successful tallies have all been in the high 80's and even the 90-mark has been breached. Roy Evans could not get near a United team that won it with 75! The bar has been raised and it would be the height of absurdity to expect it to be lowered any time soon.

So even 'coming close' can be seen as an achievement if you want it badly enough. That won't sit so well with my generation, those lucky souls who gorged on championships and European Cups in the 70's and 80's. Someone, somewhere is beginning to make their name in the game and will have the talent, the will and, yes, the money and the luck to take us to the very top. 'Settling' for Rafa does not seem quite so stupid after the results in March, April and May but a pattern has emerged over the last four years and some of us are not convinced Year Five will be any different. Of course if we had all the answers we'd be in the game ourselves, not slagging off our betters from the sidelines.

Before last season it was indisputable that Rafa was a thoroughly decent man. The occasional outburst, usually about transfer funds not forthcoming, had blotted the copybook a little bit but for most of us he was a beacon of honesty in contrast with the sewer rats he was competing with. He suddenly lost his right-hand man, Pako, and seemed all too willing to clutch at straws, even hinting at conspiracies. Given his extraordinary dignity and willingness to get on with things in his turbulent and ultimately momentous first season there was something unnerving about the change in his nature. Was he getting tougher, tired of Ferguson and Mourinho bullying and cajoling the officials and the authorities? Or was the pressure becoming too much for him? After a few months of the forthcoming season we may know more about the man. During those fairly traumatic three months after his monotonous press conference back in November he took every opportunity to tell the fans how much he loved them, the club and even the city. It became a little embarrassing if the truth were told. Once results improved he stopped doing it. When there were also one or two favourable comments about the Great Satan Hicks, there was a certain amount of disquiet amongst those fans that had marched on his behalf.

It mattered little in the end, because let's face it a winning manager can do anything he damn well pleases. Unless I haven't made myself quite clear I do believe Benitez to be incredibly talented and in the absence of an obvious replacement he fully deserves another crack at the Holy Grail. That particular description evokes memories of the Mancs and their torturous wait to get their hands on 'our' trophy. Things have come almost full circle. In chronological terms that would make Rafa our Big Fat Ron, complete with a couple of thirds a fourth and two cups, though thankfully without the long leather and the racism.

But then he did battle successfully against the two giant clubs in his own country, only to come to England and take over a club that had to read about its last title triumph in the not so recent history books. So wouldn't that make him our.........no, let's not jinx it! So much revolves around the manager at our club; there isn't another like it. Even Ferguson claimed to be jealous of the reverence Houllier received in that short period of time when we thought he was a genius. I suppose if you pull off a feat like Istanbul in your first year with such meagre materials you're entitled to a little worship, but he doesn't necessarily help matters with his constant presence pitch-side, conducting his own symphony.

Peter Robinson once said our glory days were the end product of "continuity and good players". We've still got some good players, but if we were to have continuity it would mean the Americans getting out pronto or remaining for the foreseeable future. If the players can hunker down and ignore everything going on around them (as they did in the spring) we may just see a Liverpool team challenge for the one trophy we all crave. Then smart alecs like me can be put in the stocks and routinely humiliated with rotten eggs and vegetables. If it meant eagerly awaiting text messages in April 2009 to find out how Chelsea or United are getting on, like it actually mattered to us, I'll happily take my soggy, smelly punishment. Stranger things, and all that.

Steven Kelly,
Summer 2008

Chapter 1

August

8th AUGUST

Season preview

We've spent more money so we should be more successful. Everybody tells me so. I'm prepared to spread a little sunshine this season, largely because the usual tale of woe is getting a little boring. Other fans can keep tabs on United or Chelsea's progress if they wish. I'll gauge our progress based on last season's perfunctory points total.

Where will any improvements come? Well, we know the star man can play a lot better. Our rivals' previous campaigns gathered impetus from the comforting sight of Ronaldo and Drogba pulling rabbits from hats at will. Gerrard is more than capable of this and must deliver if we are to even get close enough to choke on their exhaust fumes. Who knows, maybe we can play a full season this time and not clock off at the beginning of April. Europe is important and it's been good to us during this decade, but our gaze has to be turned inwardly. Of course the new players also need to justify the outlay. I'm sure some fans will keep defending Rafa with that hoary old chestnut about 'net spending', but only Garcia is any kind of a loss. Cisse, Bellamy and Gonzalez won't be missed in the slightest.

I can't claim to be too overwhelmed by either Torres or Babel, but maybe that's a good thing as there's little of the expectation which has clearly hampered the likes of Shevchenko. Should Rafa have the nerve to complain again about receiving insufficient backing there'll be no shortage of volunteers to pack his bags. That won't work any more. I hope we have enough cash left over to buy him a mirror. His own caution especially away from home has hampered our progress. We've matched the top two's home exploits, but once we stray from the confines of L4 our weaknesses are magnified ten-fold.

So starting from a total of 68 points last time around what can we claim to be a reasonable improvement? An extra ten? Fifteen? This is where you lose me. I just don't have the arrogance to idly speculate on what's going to happen when we reach the 80 mark. Then people turn surreal on you and twitter about those 80 points being a good 'platform' on which to build a 'challenge' for the Premiership. 90 just isn't a realistic figure and we can only do so much. We need help from outside sources.

There's a certain ironic glee when someone like Neil Warnock rests his players at Old Trafford and still gets relegated. Bryan Robson and West Brom did the same at Chelsea the year before with similar consequences. Show some backbone for God's sake. Admittedly that sort of lecture only works if Benitez himself could muster a single point at the 'big 3'. Do as we say, not as we do. We also need a challenge from Level 2, Spurs, Newcastle and their woebegone ilk. Last season Liverpool or Arsenal were not in the slightest danger of losing a top four spot despite never locating third gear.

We've profited hugely from Europe but there's definitely a shortfall in incentive. It's also a distraction. The fact that our manager and players are on much bigger bonus payments for Champions League success tells a tale. They'd have to get their act together if qualifying wasn't so predictable. How many fans actually believe all the pre-season jingoism any more? The players aren't cheap; the match tickets certainly aren't cheap. But the talk is. The new stadium plans look shiny and inspiring. Filling it will depend largely on whether we're serious about the Premiership in this and the intervening years.

Make us proud.

15th AUGUST

Aston Villa 1 Liverpool 2 (11/08/07)

Useless officials, whining opponents, infuriating players, traffic delays, overcrowded pubs, bitten nails, awful songs. Football is back. How we've missed you. It's five long years since Liverpool last won their opening game, also at Villa, but of course breaking that spell still required a few needless complications.

Several news outlets couldn't decide who the referee was. Some called him Riley and others called him Bennett. If they'd stuck to "bald and clueless" everyone could have been right. We'd begged Gerrard to raise his game this season and you can't deny it's a bright opening. We bristle when we're labelled a one-man team but sooner or later we'll have to make our peace with it, true or no. Saturday's goal had an emphatic but beautiful inevitability about it.

Villa aren't a very good side but they're precisely the sort of mid-table mediocrity we must overcome on our travels if Rafa's fourth year isn't to end with the same punctured dreams of his predecessors. It was one goal but its impact on the season could be seismic. Leaving Birmingham with a point could have had calamitous consequences. Sounds overblown I know. Would it have been fair to dismiss our chances on day one? Of course not, but what's fair about trying to be the best? Liverpool were already battling an absurd combination of huge expectation and dismissive contempt from the media.

This mountain of disrespect (exacerbated by sly attempts to add tens of millions onto Liverpool's already eye-popping budget) would only have been increased by the 88 minutes preceding Gerrard's winning strike. This was Rafa's reign in a handy bite-size chunk. Hard work and occasional glimpses of talent were undermined by a vital missing ingredient; the final finish. It's hard to take him seriously sometimes, but on Saturday his persistent gripe about adding a killer instinct to any good football we produce carried weight.

You only have to watch our players' shooting practise before the game to see how hopeless we can be. The second half was tactically spot-on but the coup de grace could never be executed. Kuyt and Torres both did good things but not the ones you expect from expensive forwards. As each chance fell to midfield and missed by ever-increasing margins a Villa equaliser loomed larger as the quality of their own football deteriorated. And it would be our ablest performer Carragher who'd gift them the opportunity. Does anyone in the world still think this infuriating sport has an ounce of logic left?

Villa fans, dancing gleefully and gurning maniacally minutes earlier, took defeat badly. Ever laughed at someone, only to trip and fall flat on your face a second later? It was a similar concoction of pain, hubris and humiliation that swept through 85% of the ground. We've never got on with them for some reason and they always seem to have a chip on their shoulders about us. Feel free to pick the irony out of that one. A few of their young bucks couldn't resist a bilious rendition of "Justice for the 39" outside, little realising some of them might be needing some 'justice' of their own if they ever show their pock-marked faces at Anfield in January. Elephants and Scousers aren't species noted for their amnesiac tendencies. A coach of ours was apparently trashed and that won't help either.

Mind you I felt like slapping a few people myself. I've made my peace, a reluctant truce if you will, with "Fields Of Anfield Road" and now there's this "Greatest Midfield In The World" nonsense. We need a Song Police, batons optional. First of all, it's not the best in the world. Secondly, it names four central midfielders and two of them weren't even playing. Thirdly, Sissoko - seriously? For some reason he came on for the last five minutes and played for Villa, breaking up every Liverpool counterattack. Not what you want when you're trying to shut the game down a second time. It's a ghastly ditty, though it scores Irony points for using the Entertainer tune.

But who quibbles after a win? Even sitting in a grimy car park for almost two hours couldn't erase the smiles. A result like this and the way it was achieved will have the optimists strutting ominously, bellowing us agnostics into a rictus-grinned submission.

Yowl at us in a week's time if you must. If you can.

22nd AUGUST
Toulouse 0 Liverpool 1 (15/08/07)
Liverpool 1 Chelsea 1 (19/08/07)

It was a week of yawn stifling. Should Liverpool players make the supreme sacrifice for St George? The media huffed and puffed, pretending anyone else cared that Carragher doesn't want to play sixth fiddle to a gaggle of stretcher cases and lightweights. And how dare Gerrard think a game with Chelsea carries more significance than England's friendly? Dungeons in the tower apparently awaited these treacherous northern monkeys.

Liverpool fans have long stopped listening to the last refuge of scoundrels. We recall how Fowler was ignored, how Redknapp was always injured and how Barnes was systematically abused. Gerrard picked up his injury during an almost comatose afternoon in Toulouse. It's to be hoped the French haven't lulled us into a false sense of security. They deserve Oscars if they have. Nice goal from Voronin, and that was about that.

Which leaves us with the umpteenth 'grudge' match with Chelsea. As predictable as a disastrous wedding in a soap opera, everyone phones in their lines for this drama-by-numbers. Rafa said this. Jose said that. "Ooooo they don't like each other do they?" On and wearily on it goes. All that's missing is Don King keeping them apart. There was a time when managers and players were club employees, brought into line if they ever dared besmirch the name of the great institutions they were fortunate enough to represent. Now cowed by the financial implications of upsetting these prima donnas boardrooms remain invisible and silent while toys fly from prams with imbecilic regularity.

Chelsea's strenuous effort to be treated as major players on the world stage goes way beyond the acquisition of star players and trophies. From tip to toe, from chief executive to deluded fans, they exude cackling pantomime odiousness designed to convince the greater clubs that their place at the table stems from something other than temporary financial engorgement. So we must stomach the lectures on what is a 'great' club and challenging for ALL trophies between the snotty remarks about our town's baser tendencies, skewered by cartoon mimicry of "de accent laaaaa". Sorry, but lopping the 'H' off History does not make you The Enemy.

We despise United for an array of reasons, shaped by experience and consecrated by time. Chelsea adopt legacy-lite, fabricating the laziest of legends, a club built almost entirely by shortcut. So why on earth is Benitez so eager to be the chump's sparring partner? He was the main antagonist before Sunday. There's no need for all this hucksterism surely? The tickets were sold weeks in advance. Does Rafa honestly think he'll get away with his oddball portrayal of LFC as minnow socialists fighting the ravenous capitalist swine? Chelsea's resemblance to Goliath can be either uncanny or illusory, but Liverpool and Benitez make a thoroughly unconvincing David. Mention Abramovich all you like but that smokescreen is becoming wafer-thin.

Take Torres for example. If we label his personal battle with Ben Haim as Gift Shop v Thrift Shop, we had the upper hand and for a while that's how it looked. We played well but we also willingly abandon whatever advantage we have. Chelsea marginally resisted the urge to do a lap of honour with their point, so it was clear which team should have won but sooner or later we have to keep supporting our forwards and we also have to keep the ball. The possession stats were ludicrous because Chelsea, as always at Anfield, were rattled and there for the taking.

Of course it never helps when the referee brings Christmas four months forward. Rob Styles never had control of the game, the penalty was scandalous and despite the simmering tedious rancour it was never a nine-card match. As Lampard celebrated someone close to me expressed relief that at least they wouldn't sing "That's why we're champions." You wouldn't have put it past them in seasons gone by, but they couldn't this time because they handed it to the other rabble last spring. If they don't needle you one way they get under your skin somehow. It's a gift of sorts.

These games are always tight so they can turn on anything marginal. Rafa's worship of "control" is futile since it can vanish in one such fraudulent moment.

Those fans that envisaged a title challenge this year will be the most disappointed while the rest of us will keep looking for signs of progression elsewhere. It's how we'll perform against the teams we're clearly superior to that will decide whether the summer outlay is ultimately justified.

29th AUGUST
Sunderland 0 Liverpool 2 (25/08/07)

A craggy Scottish manager called Jimmy Sirrell once said, "Football is about the result, everything else is just gossip." Lord knows what he would have made of mind games, 24-hour sports news channels and the internet. He'd probably shake his head in utter bewilderment at the torrent of accusations Rafa has just unleashed. We all of us have our off days but I hinted last week that there was a side of Benitez that was best kept under wraps and the pressure of having to deliver was already beginning to show.

Fears of the contempt 'Authority' has for Liverpool may have been allayed by the swift, albeit temporary, demotion of Styles. Not a bit of it: our man was just getting warmed up. The signing of Heinze from United was always going to be a tough needle to thread and some weren't entirely sure he was worth the hassle. We were trying to do business via a manager who still has the inordinate nerve to accuse anyone else of having a chip on the shoulder. As weeks stretched tediously into months the deal became more about ego and who had the greatest influence over the powers that be. So now Benitez knows. We could have told him that two months ago and saved him the trouble. We await the results of Ferguson's own 'investigation' with breath less than bated. He has assumed many guises, nearly all of them putrid, but Transfer Etiquette Lecturer? That'll be the biggest laugh of the lot.

Rafa also complained bitterly about the difference in treatment between the Mascherano and Tevez deals, while some of us would rather not dwell on the similarities, given the amount of negative attention Tevez has already attracted. And was it wise to moan about early starts when a tricky one was just around the corner? It hardly mattered, he was on a roll and there was no stopping now. Fans inevitably began to speculate on what this was all in aid of. Was it to frighten the authorities into future subservience? To rally the troops and get a little bit of that siege-mentality going? Or did he just lose it for the moment?

Once you'd read the local press slant – that these minor irritants were in fact attempts to sabotage our Premiership campaign at birth – you realised all hope of rational discourse had evaporated and that the Chauvins would be thumping their tubs with brain-splintering force. Personally I think we're better than that but we, the chilled minority, were drowned out by constant whining. So it goes.

Defeat at Sunderland would therefore have had a profoundly negative impact on our season. Thankfully they never possessed the tools to hurt us. They've always liked a bit of roughhouse up there ever since Quinn was a mere player and they still appeal for absolutely everything. On this occasion it failed to disguise a chronic lack of flair and Mark Halsey, perhaps with last week's penalty fiasco in mind, did not seem unduly cowed. Despite too many long balls early on Liverpool got to grips with the game and earned their reward from a highly unusual source.

When the ball left Momo Sissoko's boot we all did a split-second calculation where the ball would finally land. The Sea of Tranquillity was my intemperate guess. Oh we of little faith! I'd also spent the previous 30 minutes criticising Rafa for putting Momo further forward and leaving the more talented Alonso deeper. I'll end up writing the cricket column at this rate.

As at Villa we played the second half almost to perfection. It remains to be seen whether Torres can add the clinical finish that would make him one of the game's more interesting talents even at this early stage. Nerves jangled as we awaited another referee's gift to undo all the good (but incomplete) work, but it never materialised. Voronin looks useful and Babel is still finding his feet, but it's clear we now have the pace for an away strategy that has paid off handsomely thus far. Did this result spring from Rafa's midweek strop? Hardly. Sunderland will struggle manfully all season but it would have been immensely disappointing if we hadn't won, even without Gerrard.

Whether we can manage without Carragher is another matter. Let's hope he recovers soon.

Chapter 2

September

5th SEPTEMBER

Liverpool 4 Toulouse 0 (28/08/07)

Liverpool 6 Derby County 0 (01/09/07)

Okay, let's have a little quiet time. Take a few deep breaths. Consider the quality of the opposition or the number of games played and how long is left to go. I'm not getting through am I? Ten goals in a week tell their own story, and the obvious deficiencies of Toulouse and Derby don't really matter. Think back to Watford last December, when we struggled woefully against a similarly doomed side. As much as the Pessimista want to slam the breaks onto the feel-good factor something IS different about this Liverpool team. I'm almost scared to say it.

Transfer deadline day passed with little activity. Despite the hissy fit over Heinze and the broken bones of Carragher and Hyypia, Rafa decided we were okay as we were and even sacrificed Paletta. Toulouse weren't faking it in the first leg, they really were that bad. Lots of chances went begging but four were taken. That will always do for me. I'm sure when the games get harder and tighter we'll curse Kuyt's profligacy and Crouch's spongy head, but you couldn't help admiring the squad players' determination to catch the eye. Competition for places is an awful cliché but for now it seems we actually have it. Anyone not giving their all will stand out like Liberace at a fight club.

That accusation has never been levelled at Sissoko of course, it's his four-touch football that causes the consternation. So much of the game is about confidence and one goal won't make a lot of difference, but he shone with his passing as much as his work-rate. One attempt with the outside of the foot drew gasps of astonishment, not the sniggers of yore.

The Champions League draw of Marseille, Porto and Besiktas does not appear terribly difficult. Obviously many don't share my own indifference to Europe. Attending all six home games last season still wasn't enough to qualify for Athens in 70% of cases, no matter what the club subsequently claimed. Should another 'miracle' occur I've no intention of visiting Moscow anyway so I can relax and concentrate on what really matters – the Premiership.

It may be early days but we're ticking along quite nicely. Rafa may be sore after losing right-hand man Pako Ayesteran but if the club recruited Gary McAllister it would be a huge fillip for the fans. Such a good start has everyone searching for omens. Try this: wasn't Ferguson with Archie Knox for years before replacing him with someone who'd scored for them in a European final? That's me, the King of Tenuous.

Derby were there for the taking and boy, were they taken. That was hardly ever the Rafa way of old. Pako dealt primarily with the fitness of the players, one of the angriest bees in my bonnet. I bore friends to death about the night we put seven past Birmingham. Every player ran as hard in the 90th minute as they did in the first. Saturday was exactly the same. Work isn't work if you truly enjoy it. Goals, near misses and smiling faces are worth more than a hundred laps of the track. Fatigue is often in the mind. The newspapers here chose different players for man of the match. Maybe the continued absence of Gerrard is confusing the poor lambs. Yet none even mentioned the consistently excellent Finnan or the swiftly improving Arbeloa. When there are numerous candidates for star performer you know things are looking up.

Lost his assistant manager, lost Carragher, lost out on Heinze, lost Gerrard. Last season we'd have been singing "Why does it always rain on me" in funereal tones. Now we not only get on with it we chalk up our biggest league win under Benitez and go top for a few weeks. Maybe Rafa will grab his comfort blanket of caution at the first hint of danger and remember we haven't been behind yet but frankly I'm sailing in uncharted waters. I don't do 'optimistic' at the best of times, and if the light at the end of the tunnel is actually the 3.45 express service to Reality don't say you weren't warned. For the moment though it feels slightly treacherous pulling that stunt. We are playing well, end of story.

Enjoy your fortnight on cloud nine.

12th SEPTEMBER
International Week

Is there such a thing as a 50/50 relationship, where both partners love each other the same way? Or, to be cynical for a nanosecond, hold an equivalent amount of power over the other. In my experience the answer is no. You either make all the calls or you avoid them. Even when you find Ms Perfect there's always an unspoken agreement about who holds sway. It's Steven Gerrard who has turned my mind to thoughts of Love. Not an admission I'd like to get around, so keep it to yourself.

Last week our captain had his head turned by Steve McClaren. The slut. Clearly Rafa didn't want him to play for his country, nor did any sane Liverpool fan. Our objections were brusquely brushed aside. Now he didn't turn to the cameras and sneer "What you going to do about it?" but perhaps some things are best left unsaid. Who knows, maybe the toe healed suddenly and we won't hear any more about it. How likely is that though? Did Jesus return as a member of England's medical staff? Surely that would have been in the papers.

This isn't the first time I've compared our boy to Bryan Robson. Importance to club and country is without dispute but when form or fitness disappear we're both expected to collapse. Beating Derby by six proves nothing. It was only after Ferguson found other focal points and sidelined his once-greatest asset

that he ended United's interminable wait for top spot. It may
well be lunacy to suggest that Liverpool do likewise but questionable mental health has never stopped me pontificating. Ince
became their new kingpin, a controversial signing from West
Ham. Just like Mascherano, to continue the tenuous theme from
last week.

Friends accuse me of refusing to forgive our captain for his
two coquettish dalliances with Abramovich. They may have a
point. Rafa's use of injections to get the lad into the Chelsea
game hardly dealt him a winning hand in the poker game that
followed. It's the eternal conundrum for club bosses. Like all
great players Gerrard is restless and ambitious. Being the star
in one arena will never satisfy the hunger that drives him on and
thus propels us forward too. It may baffle and irk us but the fact
remains that Anfield is not the only stage.

This was also a clear demonstration of power. Ask yourself if
Crouch would act in the same manner – his Liverpool career
would be over, if it isn't already. Ferguson claimed Wayne
Rooney also asked for injections weeks ago but was refused.
After the biased Heinze verdict they hardly need to be so fastid-
ious with the FA, but whatever happened the chubster was
clearly going nowhere near the England camp. Those who view
the world through a paranoid lens might also question the
absence of Lampard and Hargreaves, given that our place in the
pecking order has been fiercely debated of late.

What isn't in doubt is that we had to watch another tedious
international, this time through our fingers, flinching every time
he kicked the ball or, more worryingly still, was kicked by an
opponent. As if England games weren't painful enough, being
expected to sit there and yell "Come on Gary John Rio Frank
Becks Joe Wayne etc" while your lunch fights for the right to
resurface. It's one of the few times we concur with our
Mancunian brethren. Passion for another team, especially one
so routinely sprinkled with failure, seems superfluous. It's not
as if the mantra "no injection necessary" was in any way reas-

suring, especially as he hobbled towards the touchline. Cramp, they said. Hmmmm, we said.

It will be weeks before we put aside all fears of an aggravated injury. Even then are we sure Rafa will forget? In Gerrard's preferred position we are ironically quite strong, and with renewed competition for places on the flanks it's not beyond possibility we could have survived without him in the short-term. The manager has spent the majority of his tenure trying to find a suitable role for our undeniably greatest talent. The nadir of this search came in Athens when player nor team-mates nor spectators seemed to understand the stratagem. Ultimately it's a team game, the sum of its parts and all that rot. Liverpool without Gerrard may be unthinkable. They said that about Bryan Robson, didn't they?

19th SEPTEMBER
Portsmouth 0 Liverpool 0 (15/09/07)

Oh well, it was nice while it lasted. After a week of squabbling over club v country how gratifying it was to see Alonso earn a ludicrous red whilst Voronin picked a needless fight with his coach. Now that's how you get along with the supporters. I know the Irish won't be best pleased with Finnan's convenient recovery. Diplomacy isn't my forte so I'll say it plain: Liverpool Come First.

I received a few catcalls on the internet regarding last week's column about Gerrard. Not enough genuflection, clearly. Unlike my Chelsea counterpart I don't actually enjoy getting on Liverpool fans' nerves so it made me examine what was written in closer detail. Using Robson for contrast got pretty short shrift. Okay, so what about United selling Van Nistelrooy and buying Carrick? United scored more goals than ever. I defy anyone to claim they knew that was a title-winning strategy. The previous year's champions added Shevchenko and Ballack. How many of us gave up the ghost there and then? Suggesting Arsenal dump Thierry Henry a year ago would have had a fresh straightjacket delivered to your door, but look where they are now. Sure it's early days but I really don't think it's madness to discuss the good of the team and question the cult of one gifted individual.

How ironic then to see my fellow countrymen seriously discussing the idea of Heskey replacing Rooney full-time and the restoration of Michael Owen as the main man before whom all others must bow after he scored twice against Russia. Four or five years ago the satellite a.k.a. Liverpool FC did not orbit around Planet Gerrard. It was Owen who was our first, last and everything. His sly defection to Spain brought numerous predictions of our decline. You could say they were somewhat wide of the mark, and while Steven's played a big part in all of that it still gets under your skin when it's suggested he carried ten others. We've got some good players here, it's about time the media showed them a little respect.

That said, their attempts to display their independence at Fratton Park left something to be desired. They were hampered by Rafa's latest squeal about the insidious plot to deny us our true greatness, and a team-sheet seemingly designed to labour the point. Internationals precede three of our longest journeys and they all have earlier starts than everyone else but that has involved three separate bodies: UEFA (international dates) the Premiership (league dates) and Sky Sports (TV schedule). They seem to have been very busy colluding behind the scenes to do us harm. Perhaps they had secret meetings at Roswell – or the book depository near Deeley Plaza.

I'd be a little more impressed with Rafa's complaints if he just once emphasised the inconvenience to the travelling fans. Short of handing him final cut over the entire fixture list I'm not sure what he expects to happen. It must be a gigantic pain in the posterior but we just have to get on with it. Sport is all about overcoming adversity, not whimpering over the slightest incursion into your preparations. You can't spend TV's money then tell them to butt out of the schedule. Beating Sunderland was the perfect response to this so-called injustice. Portsmouth are made of sterner stuff and we ought to be content with the point, especially since we didn't play too well.

Something about the team selection triggered off more than a trickle of muttering. Was it so cynical to suggest the forthcoming Porto game took priority, despite several pre-season promises that the title was our number-one target? The presence of Crouch made sense since he was fresher than the rest but his touch was understandably awry and there was little of the speed on the break that sliced through Villa and Sunderland. And let's not start on the long ball that made such an unwelcome reappearance. Heskey was not only back in the England team, he was at Fratton Park in red-shirted spirit. Late substitutions gave us straw-clutching hopes of all three points. It would scarcely have been deserved and but for Reina it could have been a lot worse.

The table still looks encouraging and the result certainly wasn't calamitous. In keeping with my chirpier countenance of late, let's wait for real strife before mongering the usual doom.

26th SEPTEMBER
Porto 1 Liverpool 1 (18/09/07)
Liverpool 0 Birmingham 0 (22/09/07)

Mockery can get you into a whole heap of trouble. We chuckled as Sam Allardyce criticised Benitez on the same day Newcastle lost to a team we've already hit for six. We guffawed as The Spesh was sent flying out of Stamford Bridge with a large boot-print on his Armani'd behind, claiming it was a mutual decision whilst still airborne. Everton's return to Europe had us rolling on the floor as the 21st Century Keystone Cops lived down to their reputation.

With tears of hilarity flowing freely it was hard to see our own season gliding with the control and fluency of Britney Spears in a car park. Which is the most successful team in football? FC Hubris. It always wins in the end. We didn't even lose to Birmingham but the murmurs of discontent grow louder. It's his fourth year in charge after huge investment in the squad. All emotions are sharpened; euphoric carnival after good wins, wailing and gnashing of teeth after draws. There are certainly plenty of drama queens around, but is he helping himself? Not really. Dropping Torres to the bench again seemed like a wilful snub to public opinion, which is obviously whipped into a frothy frenzy by the press and TV.

Rotation, they would have us believe, is spinning Benitez into an early football grave. With so many games in a short period of time it's hard to see what else could have been done. Stories that Torres is already complaining of fatigue don't help. He won't have played so much at Atletico granted, but few will sympathise with him and even less with the manager. Giving him a start against Porto (flanked by two cameo Premiership appearances) was interpreted by many as a significant statement of the manager's true priority.

We may well be entering one of the final phases of Liverpool management. We could find out the whole team had been poisoned and fans will only ask why he didn't employ another chef or taste the food himself. From now on there are no Reasons – only Excuses. Agger and Alonso are big losses at a most inconvenient time, when two games a week are the norm. Following on from Gerrard's travails does anyone seriously believe the modern football boot is up to the job? Doubtless the manager will be blamed for that too. With endorsements large and bad publicity for the product growing little or nothing will be said. Money as ever overrides common sense.

Porto saw an atrocious performance rewarded with a rather comical point. The manager's main whinge has been the lack of preparation time but with the fixtures coming thick and fast surely his own method of changing players and tactics for each game can only aggravate the situation. Once we'd played 30 minutes against Birmingham it was becoming clear that this was another fair-weather Liverpool team. All season we've looked a bit cumbersome before a goal came from nowhere, then something clicked and we proceeded to play some good football. Without the opener to build on, the confidence visibly drains away. Slowly but surely we unravel. It was ever thus with any 'work in progress'.

It certainly doesn't help when the manager thinks strikers are almost an afterthought, interchangeable and of little consequence. Selecting three different partnerships in a week is frivolous even by his standards. He picked his two pit ponies up front on Saturday and sure enough the goal threat was insubstantial bordering on transparent. If Mourinho can be shunted out for boring football and benching an expensive striker who is misfiring, what makes Rafa think he's fireproof? Especially when Torres was the dazzling highlight of such a promising start. As I've said before nothing may be what it seems on the surface but that won't help him. Hyypia admits that a manager with such a handsome track record will not change his ways. This is how he will stand or fall at Anfield no matter how much the criticism builds, but it is becoming apparent that everyone else will have to be wrong and only Benitez will be right if the long wait for the title is to end.

That doesn't seem very likely right now. The gloom before sunrise and sunset look exactly alike. We have to sit tight and see what's really happening.

Chapter 3

October

3rd OCTOBER
Reading 2 Liverpool 4 (25/09/07)
Wigan 0 Liverpool 1 (29/09/07)

May the Lord save us from the slumberfest called rotation and its discussion thereof. As a veteran of the Houllier wars I was hoping to sit this one out while the young men fight the good fight. No chance. Even when Torres is selected and scores three times it seals one worm-can shut and opens up another.

On the bench for the Premiership, starts in the Carling Cup. One fine day that straight Spanish face will break into a huge grin, revelling in the huge practical joke being played out for his own amusement. Selecting the star striker to tear Reading's reserves a new one was like visiting the corner shop in a Rolls Royce. Especially when the grubby local urchins are eager to enviously scratch their ten-foot signature in your immaculate paintwork. "We have four good strikers." No, not really. You have three decent ones; a freebie that looks like a Metallica roadie and is beginning to play like one, another that runs everywhere except into the area and the lanky one you've virtually disowned.

And then there's Torres, the quality striker you screamed and squealed for all those long noisy months ago. The four are not on the same level at all. Rafa manages teams like Hitchcock made films. The master of suspense famously called actors "cattle" and claimed to lose interest once he'd finished the storyboards in his office. He'll deny it till he's purple in the face but maybe the boss is finding the elevation of Torres by supporters and the press rather tiresome.

Aided and abetted by poor officials Reading's bit-part shamateurs roughed up our boy with overzealous borderline bullying. Torres dusted himself down and simply became more determined to score. Having previously seen off John Terry's putrid attempt at intimidation in August he wasn't to be coerced by the bargain basement varieties. It still wasn't enough to keep Rafa quiet. On brief sojourns from his day job of putting the whole football world to rights he occasionally likes to manage Liverpool. Is it just me or is he becoming a bit of a bore on the quiet? Internationals, TV interference, protecting 'quality' players (despite Fernando fending for himself more than adequately), all can be put right by our man if only the authorities would listen.

He has his allies of course; something about fighting our corner and ensuring we're not treated like suckers in the coming months. To the uninitiated it just sounds like one never-ending complaint. Again we get the big speech about having everyone fresh for next spring. All well and good if there's still something to play for then. Last spring everyone was fit as a fiddle and ended up just playing in the European matches! Logic no longer resides in these parts.

It's not as if we've not started well but something is clearly not right. It reminds me of Houllier before his blip, when our record was even better (nine wins, three draws) without ever convincing anyone we had the necessary title credentials. It all seems rather illusory. Discount the thrashing of Derby and we're averaging a goal a game in the league. Yes, point at the Mancs' current standing if you wish. Winning ugly is fine and dandy when they do it, obviously. Carlos Tevez couldn't really do otherwise I suppose.

Beating Wigan can't eradicate all doubt. Doing it whilst playing badly is the mark of champions, say those who forget they said exactly that just before Houllier drove Liverpool over a cliff. Nothing impairs eyesight more than three points. Wigan took defeat badly, especially in a corner of the stadium where they outnumbered Liverpool fans 100-1. Coincidentally they'd made their peace with the disappointment once 5,000 Scousers came out of the away section to politely inquire about their 'fists first' policy. It was another journey home tinged with relief. It's hard to calibrate such games because even if Wigan play out of their skin and we stink victory is still expected.

Benayoun had himself a good week, with favourable comparisons to Garcia. Wigan quietly fumed about the officials. Rafa after his Reading tirade for once chose discretion and ignored the physical excesses of several Pieland players, Michael Brown especially.

We won so an excuse wasn't needed and no one even mentioned r*t*t**n. He can spin on his chin with a fish in both ears as long as we win.

10th OCTOBER
Liverpool 0 Marseille 1 (03/10/07)
Liverpool 2 Tottenham 2 (07/10/07)

Marseille was the accident waiting to happen. It had been coming for weeks. With fans' unique gift for rationalisation some greeted the result as proof that Liverpool were finally making the Premiership a priority. Surely the selection of Leto, Sissoko and Crouch was the biggest indication yet that Rafa was in tune with the majority of the support. Well, that's what we wanted to think.

The instant deification of any Liverpool boss and his own constant references to "control" means every kick, flick and tic at Anfield becomes part of some shrewd, omnipotent masterplan. The truth is more unsettling: Rafa probably believed that team and those tactics could get the job done. The end product was as eyeball-splintering as anything from Houllier's time. Yes, that bad. There was an almost arrogant disregard for the opposition and not for the first time. Previous calamities at home to Grazer and CSKA were cited as everyone fled from our deathly silent (ahem) 'cauldron'. It's important to remember other bad times since the last only seems like the worst. Just as thrashing Derby unleashed the sort of communal mania associated with triumphal homecomings of all-conquering heroes, so losing to Djibril and his pals had every lemming looking for the nearest cliff.

This schizophrenia entertains the fans of other clubs and fuels the media machine. Cautious optimism in victory and quiet unease in defeat simply aren't sexy enough. They are terribly, terribly dull in fact but no less required. We started badly and got worse, just as we did in Portugal, so team selection can't be the fall guy forever. We played so deep I'm sure Torres appealed for offside at one point. Crouch has had all the joy and ingenuity sucked from his elongated bones. It was lucky that our old mate Cisse remains as annoyingly insubstantial as ever but even his 12th-man presence couldn't save us.

Ironies abound, raising uncomfortable parallels with Houllier's failures. Baros didn't work out, nor did Morientes. Cisse left, so did Bellamy, while Kuyt's impression of Heskey (fifth midfielder disguised as second striker) is unerringly accurate. Each time the player cops the flak while the manager shrugs and looks as bewildered as the rest of us. They showed the urgency in the final minutes that might have mattered in the opening portion of the game. Too little, way too late.

The loss of Ayesteran has caused concern as little has gone right since but it also coincided with the international break, in particular Gerrard's defiance. He's been so poor since returning. Under pressure to provide answers Rafa's starting to sound quirky, claiming players were running more, covering more ground and in "fantastic" physical condition. Really? From what I saw last Wednesday we look shattered already. Carragher's still not 100% yet and Hyypia wasn't meant to be playing so much. We'll maintain a diplomatic silence over the woeful passing and the 90-minute wait for a shot on target.

He'll stick to his guns and many will love him for it because only in football and politics is the recuperative power of pig-headedness held in such high esteem. When you look at the gaggle of ex-players who earn a living telling managers where they're going wrong it must be tempting to ignore their and my ill-informed squeals and circle the wagons. It has to be said though, that broken watches tell the right time twice a day and this could well be one of those moments.

It's not as if we played that badly against Spurs but in the face of freakish adversity we crumbled to dust and Torres' late equaliser didn't erase the travesty of the 40 minutes that followed Keane's second. It was painful to watch. With Kuyt on the wing and Babel up front you were completely deafened by the 40,000 'pings' of patience snapping. Even the continually ragged performance of our centre-halves feels like the end product of putting all our eggs in one basket over Heinze. However, some players are letting us down badly. The new lads are entitled to look like rabbits in the headlights. Those who've been here throughout the decade aren't. Standing up to be counted? The likes of Riise are lying on their belly right now.

Let's hope the next internationals disrupt the current 'flow', just as they did in September.

17th OCTOBER
International Week

It never rains but it pours, so they say. Whilst our woes could scarcely be called torrential and a flood warning would be hysterical in the extreme there is a tiny yet discernible trickling around the ankles. You half expect Rafa to sing a bar or two of that miserable Travis song at every press conference nowadays. He'll be starting his own scapegoat farm soon.

Moaning about another international break raised eyebrows skywards. Not this nonsense again, we thought. Then Torres tore something or other – in a training session for added ire – and we all joined in on harmonies and percussion. I see Robbie Keane missed a golden chance for Ireland from more or less the same spot he scored against us. Twice. Somebody up there is rubbing it in a tad. Harping on about obstacles tends to become a self-fulfilling prophecy. I admit this is a bit hypocritical coming from one of the world's foremost miserablists. Observing life from beneath a cloak of suffocating darkness is meant to dilute the pain and disillusionment of a long-suffering football fan. Forewarned is forearmed et cetera. I'm here to tell you this is a steaming wave of horse fumes. Those who had a tiny inkling our good start was a mere deception still feel as deflated and bemused as the suckers who fell for it.

International week should have brought a period of calm reflection, but if anything it's made matters worse and the arguments get fiercer, with uncanny echoes of 2002-03, when it began to go spectacularly wrong for the previous regime. Early optimism dashed, Gerrard in poor form, unforeseen struggles in Europe (thanks to Rafa's Valencia, bizarrely) and a manager with an escalating excuse count. It's a cycle as old as the seasons. Out of the next five league games four are traditionally difficult: Everton, Blackburn and Newcastle away plus a rejuvenated Arsenal at home. Try and find anyone remotely looking forward to that little lot.

Interestingly enough Monsieur Henry has now admitted that his presence may have been one of the stifling factors in Arsenal's recent failures. When I suggested Gerrard might be doing likewise at Anfield I was called amongst other things a certain part of the female anatomy – and I don't mean eyelash. While amateur psychologists search for reasons why he's playing badly it was hardly a comfort to note he stinks just as pungently for England. Living in Rumour City it isn't possible for a footballer to simply have a bad run of form of course, but never fear everybody, Harry Kewell's on his way back. When fans are banking on the one footballer that makes Louis Saha look like Lazarus there can surely be no more straws in the world left to hold onto.

I raised a topic on my fanzine's website about what Reds expected this season, given we'd spent no small sum. It was obvious most respondents would emphasise the league, citing the realistic hope of competing for first place by next spring even if it turned out to be a forlorn one. We've only done this three times in 16 years, which frankly is risible for a club of this size. Evans just about managed it twice and Houllier preserved our dreams until the last week of April 2002. This discussion evoked further reminiscences about the calamitous season that followed. Moores eventually kept Le Boss on but tellingly denied him any significant funds to do the job properly. Understandable perhaps given the purchases of Diouf, Diao and Cheyrou the previous summer – but why keep a manager if you don't trust him to spend your money?

So those 50 million or so Euros given to Benitez will become extremely important in the coming months. I suspect this will be the first of many references to that figure. Billionaires tend not to be frivolous with their hard-earned cash, and our American owners have gone conspicuously quiet of late. If the gap between the top and us continued to grow discussions about the future will build and build, in my experience getting nastier the longer it drags on.

No doubt I'll be asked again if I've ever managed at the highest level. I haven't, in case you were wondering. I've also forgotten what I said the last three times this 'argument' was put to me. Something tells me I'd better refresh my memory – and fast.

24th OCTOBER
Everton 1 Clattenburg 2 (20/10/07)

What's Spanish for "get out of jail" or "daylight robbery"? While my Mancunian colleague opens his bumper book of quips let's crack on. Even by derby standards, where sanity seldom prevails, Saturday was weird.

Abandoning previous attempts to twinkle toe our way through the Goodison minefield Rafa packed his team with sloggers: two holding midfielders and two workaholic 'forwards'. All fine and dandy once you avoid silly mistakes like, say, putting the ball in your own net. The best laid plans et cetera. Watching Sami is like seeing footage of an old lion in one of those crummy East European zoos. It breaks your heart and if Everton weren't so chronically devoid of creativity and adventure it could have been a lot worse. One shot on target, and we gave them that. The atmosphere was what bigoted outsiders expect of us, a glutinous mix of savagery and sentiment. A half-time plea to fight gun crime in the city was met with warm applause but didn't stop Blues calling us "murderers" and reds screaming "Munich" at Neville. Classy.

Cleaner fun was to be had at the expense of Everton's supermarket benefactors and a move to a new stadium outside the city limits. They've made so much pernicious use of their Scouserdom over the years that there was little comeback to our taunts. The second half exploded with the sort of mayhem only football provides. We'd spent the first half complaining about Lescott fouling Finnan, and how even a peripheral England figure can get away with anything. Then our own untouchable strode forward and turned the whole afternoon on its head.

It looked a penalty all right but a theatrical flourish never hurts. Too much was made of Clattenburg's yellow/red dilemma, much as it was when Styles was similarly 'confused' with Essien back in August. Both men eventually made the right decision, a fact largely ignored in the frenzied rush to skewer officials on the technology spit. "Gerrard told him to send Hibbert off." Read that sentence aloud and realise the enormity of the accusation being made.

At 1-1 against ten men there was a sudden feeling we could win this game. Hardly a "Eureka!" moment but it certainly hadn't been there for the preceding 47 minutes. Should the disappearance of Tony Hibbert really instigate such a turnaround? Even then Rafa kept his workers on the pitch whilst discovering belatedly he was allowed to replace his captain. We've seen numerous games where such action was warranted. This wasn't one of them, but it gave a precipice frisson to an already frenetic fixture. "If we don't win now he'll be absolutely slaughtered" was the general consensus around me, although not couched in such delicate phrases. As the woeful Sissoko finally made way for Pennant in the 88th minute it seemed late and desperate. It was more than convenient that Gerrard's replacement Lucas eventually provided another key moment and Rafa broke with tradition to step foot on the turf to congratulate the players.

Given the firestorm that would have greeted a draw he was perhaps entitled to savour the moment but it was one more oddity to pile on top of the others. There was something inevitable about the aftermath, ceaseless blue complaint about all decisions. They might have a case this time around but the blue boys have cried wolf so often it's hard to take them seriously any more. In 2006 we had Gerrard sent off after 10 minutes. We won 3-1. One of the managers went to the press to complain about the referee. He wasn't Spanish. Moyes was in full neck-vein-popping mode as usual, listing at least five conspiracies and describing Kuyt's misguided leap near Neville as "four feet off the floor". What is this, The Matrix? His comments about Clattenburg were scandalous. Pipe down man, you're pathetic. It's not your job to make Neil Warnock look good.

It's all a smokescreen Everton have hidden behind for the vast majority of the last four decades. They'll never change. I doubt Carragher had sufficient energy left to drag down a lump like Lescott but since he also sprinted 70 yards to the away end in five seconds flat to celebrate victory I might be wrong there. We had the points, the Blues had faces like thunder and were preparing for their annual communal bleat.

Just another day by the Mersey.

31st OCTOBER

Besiktas 2 Liverpool 1 (24/10/07)
Liverpool 1 Arsenal 1 (28/10/07)

We knew that Everton's reaction to last week would be bad, but they surpassed themselves. When they move to the outskirts every Red will need a doctor's appointment simply to confirm we haven't gone deaf.

Moyes whined about snubbing an apology Clattenburg had no intention of making, while the poor dears revelled in the belief they'd got him banned from the Premiership – only to discover he had a UEFA Cup match and was due a break! Since he is apparently in the pay of LFC perhaps he was just another victim of Rafa's rotation system? We could have used him in Turkey. A goal down and with little creativity a pen and a red card would have been useful.

Even via the small screen the Besiktas atmosphere was unbelievable. The hardy souls who went insisted TV did it little justice. We flatter ourselves in this country that we're a passionate bunch. Sure, we can turn it up on demand but most English games are played in pin-drop silence by comparison. Defeat meant more reminders of Houllier. It was a Gerrard substitution and public criticism back then that first raised the eyebrows of Le Boss' acolytes. Rafa's own response to his Goodison bombshell could have been short and sweet: "We won, Lucas provided the key moment" but his fetish for justification and an overpowering desire to let everyone see his cleverness held sway, like a visible puppeteer. The heart's passion, the head's control. In Rafaworld only one can prevail, and it is something he cannot get to grips with: he needs it all. He surely wasn't complaining when his captain ran 60 yards for the equalising penalty.

Poor Sami was lax again in Turkey. It looks bad but he wasn't meant to play so much. The impact of Agger's injury has been staggering. His and Alonso's reputations have swelled in their absence. At a similar rate of invisible improvement Kewell will be greeted like the lovechild of Pele and Maradona if he ever returns. It looks all over in Europe. Those of us not in thrall to the continental experience can shrug and yawn, Rafa and the new owners clearly cannot. Newspapers filled pages with 'concern' for the manager's future. The hitherto silent Hicks felt moved to offer verbal support after months of silence. Such ignorance of English custom provided rare humour. Tom probably had to ask afterwards why a vote of confidence is "dreaded". He also revealed the new ground has somehow added £100 million to its already eye-watering cost. In 2000 fans were railroaded into the idea of moving from our spiritual home by the original £80 million asking price. It has increased five-fold since then and still no work has begun. It beggars belief that we can pay it all back. Arsenal are dangled as our role model but numerous titles and sublime football played their part and even there it's still a case of "so far, so good".

We've admitted that ticket prices will rise, probably steeply. If it's to watch some of the stodgy rubbish served up in the league this decade I can envisage a few people declining future invitations. Chelsea's weekend demolition of City put our September euphoria into perspective. United and Arsenal are also playing some excellent stuff. Liverpool? At times we've looked like deep-sea divers exploring an ocean of treacle. 'Laboured' is underplaying it a tad.

The current form of both sides dictated Sunday's events. It didn't need a crystal ball to predict our tactics. Now we've got TWO forwards as makeshift wingers! We obviously showed tremendous character, exuding plenty of the passion that does have a role in the Rafa masterplan after all. It almost worked, but the longer it went on the more ragged we became. No amount of effort could knock Arsenal out of their passing stride. Before long it resembled the night we beat Arsenal's untouchables in 2004.

Three years later we need a similar policy to thwart a team we've pipped to third place twice, allowing them to run the show at a ground they hate. And we didn't win. The means weren't justified by the end, and if rotation was designed to maintain fitness how come we're suddenly dropping like flies? Perhaps there is a language where this can all be translated as Progress – but English isn't it. Let's call it Desperanto in our wacky Scouse way.

Chapter 4

November

7th NOVEMBER
Liverpool 2 Cardiff 1 (31/10/07)
Blackburn 0 Liverpool 0 (03/11/07)

Maybe we should all wean ourselves off cup football? Having somehow persuaded the public to pay high prices for reserve matches in all but name, United upped the stakes in scandalous fashion by extracting money from people's accounts in advance for games they weren't actually interested in. Either that or lose your tickets for the games that really matter. Liverpool as ever waddle wearily after the gravy train, late as usual, but no doubt will clamber onboard eventually, citing their "in order to compete" mantra that reveals another con is looming. Whenever someone asks how many are on the season ticket waiting list it grows by another 10,000. It makes you wonder if they're just keeping us all on a tight leash.

The game with Cardiff wasn't bad, gilded by another chance to let Fowler feel the love. Their fans had the usual quota of lower league giddiness from breathing the rarefied Premiership air and a few little skirmishes in and around the ground marred the occasion. El Zhar scored a screamer but our younger players rarely look like stepping up. Not that they're likely to get a chance in important games, just these glorified training sessions.

In the nineties our comparatively chilled approach to youth still supplied several key performers. Since we've built modern facilities and adopted an international scouting system, no one has come through. Carragher and Owen starred in the Youth Cup win of 1996. They scored on their debuts for the first team within a year and were regulars within two. Gerrard soon followed. Something about wells running dry springs to mind despite dominating the Youth Cup in the last two years. We can laugh at United flotsam like O'Shea and Fletcher, but it saved them money to put towards quality and nobody will convince me we haven't had players on a similar level this decade. Add the prices of the Houllier and Rafa mini-failures that we casually call chickenfeed and it mounts up to a none-too-pretty penny.

Everyone must have seen the infamous Riise pay-slip on the internet by now, whilst stifling nauseous groans of incredulity. Stephen Warnock hasn't exactly discredited the decision to release him but if his mere presence was making Riise shape up we should have kept him. Competition for places is an admirable concept but it doesn't appear to be working for us. We knew we couldn't just stroll onto Blackburn's patch and dictate terms but few expected those tactics. Gerrard roaming and Kuyt slogging away forlornly was exactly what we did to Kaka's boys. We gave Blackburn the same respect as Milan! In fact we gave them more because at least Alonso has a creative streak, unlike Sissoko whose interpretation of 'pass and move' seems to be 'pass to an opponent' and 'move backwards to avert the impending danger'.

There is little intuition in our play but does rotation explain everything? Kuyt plays as much as Gerrard but the moment they almost collided six yards from goal brought new meaning to the word Farce. Kewell, who learned his trade under other managers, showed more control and guile in 20 minutes than Babel will show in a lifetime if he remains under the tutelage of this manager. Why did it take so long to raise the temperature? Cynics claim the earlier Arsenal-United draw affected things but surely the chance to gain ground should have been grasped tighter. We're virtually the home side at Ewood Park anyway but the masses were subdued, smothered into silence by an approach bordering on cowardice until late on.

This is where Rafa will lose the supporters, that emphasis on what the opposition does rather than what we can do. It's no use buying Babel or Benayoun if the fear of risk paralyses them. The late charge has emerged so often this season you wonder if they'd sell you tickets for the final 15 minutes at a discount. Of course there's a case to be made for a significant improvement once Agger, Alonso and Torres come back. The table does not look too bleak and the next four games are winnable. The performances though are troubling. The number of fans who believe the absentees will make a difference while the team shows such little courage is dwindling.

With Jol out of White Hart Lane the press need a new wicker man. Small wonder Rafa can smell burning but there's only one man who can douse the flames.

14th NOVEMBER
Liverpool 8 Besiktas 0 (06/11/07)
Liverpool 2 Fulham 0 (10/11/07)

See what happens, when you let the opposition worry about you for a change? The situation in Europe still looks bleak of course. The mauling of Besiktas could well make Porto and Marseille more cautious than we need them to be but anyone complaining about eight goals is in serious danger of losing the little joie de vivre they ever had.

It's great hearing the experts denigrate the Turks' admittedly lax defence. Funnier still to hear the Rafalytes claim we didn't do anything different tactically from previous matches! Throughout this tournament's history giants have faced 'minnows' and no one else has scored that many. Arsenal and United get seven? Attacking master-class. Liverpool score eight? Defensive catastrophe. So it goes. I'm usually the ringleader of the "go on, impress me" gang but would a little credit kill them? Commentators urging Rafa to smile completely miss the point. This is serious business. He's not a game-show host. Ignore too those who bleat about events in Turkey a fortnight before. They're the Nouveaux with no history to fall back on. When football becomes an exact science it'll be time to take up crocheting.

Such disparity is not uncommon. Liverpool's last title winners put nine past Palace but they still knocked us out of the cup. We also put eight past Swansea after drawing away. What's logic ever had to do with it? If the referee confused his sports and TKO'd Besiktas at half time we couldn't have complained. Goals, near misses, woodwork glanced, desperate tackles, a frazzled goalkeeper: airtight evidence of a team finally unshackled. I dislike the 'superfans' who sneer at their inferiors and utter that fatuous cliché, "you want entertainment – go to the circus." Last week was how it ought to be, used to be and can be again if the manager only realised his own potential and that of his players. If ever you hear the words "football boss who plays chess", simply grab the nearest bludgeon and knock yourself out or wait for the 'football' to do it for you.

The second half was a wonderful bonus, the result of a shift in ambition that has been too long in coming. Accuse me of embroidering the theory somewhat but there does seem to be a karmic reward for adventure. Deflections fly in, saves fall to the nearest Liverpool player, decisions suddenly go in your favour. You think that's fanciful? Watch any game at Old Trafford and we'll talk further. Gerrard's back in good form while Hyypia and Carragher have raised their game from a curiously low level. It's great Sami found a second wind from somewhere. Legend isn't a word to be bandied about lightly, especially for someone without a league medal, but in Hyypia's case I'll gladly make an exception.

Not that Fulham or Besiktas gave him much to do. In a way Saturday was the better result, a triumph of persistence over stiffer resistance. Thank God Rafa still has a sense of fun and occasion. He last picked an unchanged team when he was on the brink of 100 rotations, then hands in a duplicate team sheet for his 200th game in charge! How he must have relished the irony when our fortunes turned once he made some changes. The visitors were unnervingly comfortable, and it's one of our biggest flaws that the clock needs to tick louder before we show the required urgency.

Some fans take comfort from a decent performance but the rest realise it's a results-driven business. Another two points dropped at home, however unluckily, and a howl of derision out of proportion with our position would have woken the dead. It was great to put one over on Lawrie Sanchez, a man I've despised since 1988 and who has dined out on that goal ever since. He's another of these two-bit managers who can only blame officials when things go wrong, and his assessment of Torres' goal as a mishit was ludicrous.

Niemi meanwhile paid the ultimate price for refusing to acknowledge the traditional Kop welcome. He's not the only one nowadays. In a sport plagued by ill-mannered braggarts and impossibly poor losers it seems churlish and reckless to chip away at one of the few remaining acts of sportsmanship in the game.

21st NOVEMBER
International Week

I'm indebted to the kind soul who inquired after my health recently. Fears arose because of a marked difference in the column. "You seemed upbeat, optimistic, almost...happy. Sure you're okay?" Everyone's a comedian these days.

If you can't smile when your team scores eight then further opportunities for merriment will be rarer than hens' teeth. Besides, there's nothing like an international week to slap you back down to reality. It's so, so dull. I won't bore you with the "Liverpool as a separate state, the unofficial capital of Ireland" speech again. Frankly, I'm not terribly bothered about your lot either. One's teenage years are the most formative of your life, and back in the 70's England failed to qualify for three consecutive tournaments as the Reds swept all before them. There was no choice to make. For the uber-patriots it was bleak back then. Imagine how that would play now, amidst the media overload and tabloid shriekathon of today. The shamed coach would no doubt be required to commit hara-kiri, preferably with a rusty fork on live television in order to satisfy the crazed bloodlust of those who truly believe England still rules the waves.

There are certain similarities to the big four. A manager cannot cite injured players or bad luck, even when there's a glut of both. You're expected to WIN and nothing should stand in your way. Not that McClaren filled anyone with confidence from day one. As with players, limited opportunities for 'our' managers are entirely the fault of Jonathan Foreigner esquire it would seem. You'll get nowhere by reminding such fools that England were a lot poorer in the days when the worst crimes against the language were committed by Kenny Dalglish. A period of calm will prevail since there's no chance of Croatia blocking England's fortuitous path to Switzerland. It's a sign of football's moral vacuity that some thought Israel v Russia would be a stitch-up thanks to Abramovich's 'generosity'. We really do believe the worst nowadays.

In Liverpool there were futile attempts at livening up the week, and it was hardly a surprise that they involved Gerrard. He had to explain a thoughtless remark about England being 'bigger' than us, which was inevitably twisted in a variety of ways. He's not my favourite person and I've been chastised more than once for things said on this page, but there comes a time when you can't blame him for all the woes of the world. Yes, his remark about foreign players was inconsiderate to the majority of men he's supposed to be leading, and of course his manager. I don't think he's callous, just self-absorbed and a bit thick. He'd have been better off keeping quiet, especially as his decision to play with a broken toe in September played a part in our loss of momentum.

Now he's back in form our prospects look rosier, and there are enough outsiders driving wedges wherever they can without adding to them. The two main men at Anfield both suffer from fans' double-shyness once bitten. Whenever we're cautious Rafa is plagued by comparisons to Houllier, and if Gerrard shows the slightest bit of patriotism he's Owen mark 2. Some of Rafa's tactics are boring, but Gerrard has one crucial difference over Michael; he stayed. What's happened to Owen since might be the single greatest example of karma ever. Even a year ago news of another injury would have had me rolling on the floor in ghoulish synchronicity. Not in pain, merely in stitches.

Boredom made me dig out a tape of his first 100 goals for Liverpool and I admittedly started to mellow. Roy Evans was insisting as early as 1998 that he had to be treated like a glass sculpture if his career wasn't to end prematurely. The tape played on and there was the boy king, arms aloft sparking bedlam at the Millennium after slotting his second past David Seaman. I don't get teary too often but the occasional lump in the throat will not betray the macho code. Now look at him; despised by his former worshippers, disliked and distrusted by perennial screw-ups Newcastle, unable to play consecutive games without shattering into fragments.

Only a heart of reinforced concrete could fail to break at the sight.

28th NOVEMBER
That press conference (22/11/07)
Newcastle 0 Liverpool 3 (24/11/07)

Those idiots who said England were a certainty for Euro 2008 – how stupid must they feel, eh? Feeling no desire for omniscience I fully admit Croatia made me look a fool last week. We're not talking McClaren-stupid, just enough for me to avoid rash predictions in future.

The hysteria here gets worse. Forget an entire first-choice defence and attack was missing while the goalkeeper and Gerrard were indescribably awful. This was a night of shame and infamy and that's that. I could claim to have jinxed England deliberately. It's a ploy we regularly use on the website, predicting 3-0 wins to the opposition however feeble. It got us to Istanbul. Rafa and the boys played their part and it didn't seem so funny at halftime in the Ataturk, but our role in the triumph was wiped from the history books. That's hurtful.

We revived the tactic for Newcastle and it worked a treat. My prediction said they'd beat us thanks to own goals by Benitez, Gillett and Hicks – a feeble joke but many a true word etc. It's another example of the Rafa standoff and it's become tedious. One wondered earlier on whether he'd have the nerve to cite insufficient funding, although he later claimed they've stopped him acquiring free players. How likely is that, though? It possibly centres on Mascherano, a player often ignored during transfer speculation since some think he's already accounted for. Words, some unpleasant, passed between the owners and the manager, sparking a press conference that made Houllier look like a poster boy for good mental health.

Almost every question received the same robotic response, apart from the bizarre interest in the England job. Was that to get the fans onboard? The Charge of the Light Brigade was a less catastrophic strategy. Heads were scratched less feverishly once the Americans released their statement, but puzzlement was simply replaced by concern. So we're back to this: another club interested in Rafa's services, worries about financial backing, and implicit threats back and forth across the ocean. And just when things are beginning to look good.

As a teenager I was devastated by Shankly's departure. It was only in adulthood we learned how the great man bullied and blustered to get his own way until the club finally accepted his oft-offered resignation. If we could do that to Shankly what makes Rafa thinks he's secure? The owners are easy targets since they've no page in our history. They're already open to accusations that net spending on players hasn't improved under their tenure, but too many fans want zillions spent without rhyme or reason, then shrug their shoulders at the cost of the new stadium with no real idea how such startling amounts can be recouped. This isn't Monopoly we're playing.

So conspiracy theories abound. Was he forcing the club to dump him so he could take a payoff and move to Munich? Having been publicly admonished and told to concentrate on coaching, Benitez turned up at Newcastle in a tracksuit! Had he finally flipped? Or was the Champions' League crest a pop at that crass loudmouth Allardyce? Either way it was hardly proof of unflinching focus on the task in hand. Did Sissoko replace Mascherano to show how much we'd miss the latter if he were relinquished?

Once the game began all the political and psychological non-sense evaporated. We were superb again. The opposition will be derided, what we now call Besiktas Syndrome, where Liverpool can never beat good teams but only rubbish ones. The abuse of Gerrard was bewildering. Newcastle suffer because of Owen's England obsession, yet they boo another player who ensured the littlest backstabber has to concentrate on club duty for once. Torres had himself a strange afternoon. His admirers in Madrid warned us that his finishing could be eccentric but never prepared us for this. Another 8-0 would have flattered but only slightly. The sounds of discontent and chaos are never truly stifled at St James Park, and it never fails to satisfy when the Reds have made things even worse.

So round 2 to Rafa clearly, but a knockout blow? Hardly. The rumble goes on. He says he will "keep winning games for my supporters". We're not yours, as we weren't Shankly's. We're Liverpool's. Something you'd do well to remember before it's too late. Liverpool fans always expect negative headlines when the team starts to play well. We often circle the wagons and blame media mischief. No such luxury this time. This is a mess almost entirely of our own making, although stories of Rafa being sacked soon must surely be nonsense?

When he tugged at the heartstrings earlier in the week about "my" club, "my" players and even "my city" it did seem out of character for one often accused of being a cold fish. Now it looks more like the first public punch in a fight that looks set to continue becoming bloodier by the day. The repetition of the phrase "coaching my players" made him sound like the deranged computer in '2001'.

Then came the humiliating slap down from Hicks about sticking to coaching. The words "it's what you're good at" were presumably erased from the final version, but the message was devastatingly clear. Had they checked his record with Valencia? With a less hands-on approach in transfer policy he won two titles in three years. Or were the owners annoyed with another bout of foot-stamping only six months after his Athens outburst and three months after buying £50 million's worth of new players?

This isn't just about finalising contracts for 'free' players, of that we're certain. Something is fundamentally wrong, and the man who has kept quiet throughout – Rick Parry - may yet emerge as the key figure in all of this.

Chapter 5

December

5th DECEMBER
Liverpool 4 Porto 1 (28/11/07)
Liverpool 4 Bolton 0 (02/12/07)

So that's it? No sacking, no resignation, no-one run out of town? You lose count of the times football does this to you. Sound and fury, signifying nothing as usual. It's like a bad soap opera. Betrayals and crises everywhere, then back to normal in an instant, then more chaos. The same old plots regurgitated. You're better off standing back, biding your time and sifting through the debris – if there is any. And if you question reports like "sacking imminent", people tap their nose and wink, citing "behind the scenes talks" or saying, "wait and see, it's still simmering." Whatever.

I saw the fans' protest march last Wednesday. All very noble of course, but I'm at an age where beer and warmth are comforting and addictive. I'm afraid I didn't join the on-line petition either. Getting to be quite the company man! I wouldn't sign anything that referred to Rafa as "the best since Paisley". You always see that ungrateful little snub to Dalglish. It often happened under Houllier too.

Am I the only Liverpool fan on the planet who hasn't forgotten that press conference where Rafa gave the same answer 25 times, then touted for another job? Some fans' reaction to the owners – basically one of "Spend your money but keep your noses out" – has been incredibly naïve. I'll bet it's the same people who pleaded with Moores to sell in the first place. The press had free rein, as if they actually needed any assistance. Once the floodgates open they can write anything and be believed. Had aliens taken Liverpool over? Hence Rafa's robotic repetition. The little green man inside him having acclimatisation problems, perhaps?

Hicks was always the more voluble of the two since they 'bought' us. A link to Roma seems to have gone quiet, but if Rafa pipes up again and this guy thinks he's John Wayne something's got to give. Sealing the deal for Mascherano might be the next battleground. You hear things like everyone else, but I hate speculation and can happily wait for, y'know, 'news'. Let the constant chitter-chatter wash over you. All it does is highlight grievances. Heard the one about Rick Parry 'forgetting' to tell the owners Rafa's transfer needs? It's believable to those who bear a grudge after Athens and wanted Parry out anyway. Didn't Gerrard claim Parry also stalled on his contract after Istanbul? Ah, see? No smoke without fire, put two and two together etc. All of it tiresome, because unless you're on the inside you can't know.

With mutiny in the air and jobs on the line it was hardly surprising there was anxiety on the pitch. That would explain the players' poor passing, although Porto's technique helped to highlight it. I'd never say the ground was quiet but it wasn't the widely predicted wall of sound. The Kop was noisy enough, but observing from the geriatrics stand it didn't spark a similar flame of resistance elsewhere. Perhaps as the oldest of the old school, they weren't prepared to fully exonerate Benitez for his share of the blame after a week's worth of panic. If the manager needed ammunition in his funds war, he got it from Torres. He was surreal at Newcastle but against Porto and Bolton he produced the sort of finish that separates the special from the proficient. While everyone else seemed ready to canonise Rafa the old guard around me muttered about the time it took to get Crouch on. Never satisfied, overly critical, sullen - I'd found my spiritual home!

Liverpool have scored 21 goals in the five games since that excruciating visit to Blackburn. We begged Rafa to unshackle his team and by God he has responded magnificently. Winning cures all ills. If he wanted to paint the owners' faces on his buttocks, then treat the press to the world's creepiest ventriloquist act, he could probably get away with it now. Bolton had already roughed up United the week before and certainly wouldn't be the manager's favourite opposition, but they barely got a sniff on Sunday. Can we now look forward to a week's peace and quiet then? Let's hope so, but antagonising a filthy-rich employer isn't something they'll forget and your team cannot win forever. They can always bide their time.

Ask Jose Mourinho.

12th DECEMBER
Reading 3 Liverpool 1 (08/12/07)

So run that shortlist of candidates by us again. Fickle? Me? Because if last night in Marseille was anything like as bad as it was at Reading, and the visit of the Devil's own spawn produces its usual grotesque charade at the weekend, we could be looking for a new manager.

That's how modern football works, doesn't it? A week is a long time in politics, an eternity in this most impetuous of games. It's a mark of our club's importance that certain names already thrown into the mix are also being linked to the England job. Capello and Klinsmann were two of the stranger names, but none can surpass the surreal outrage of the whispers concerning Jose Mourinho. Surely this is never going to happen? It's not even about clauses inserted in the Chelsea payoff to The Spesh, but the thought of such muddled thinking within the Anfield hierarchy; "Let's get rid of that loudmouth Benitez and get the shy gracious yes-man with the grey hair and the wavy lip." Mind you, with Parry involved...

Look, it's all sensationalist short-term garbage. You know it and I know it, but I've tired of the struggle. It's actually feels good to give up on archaic customs like patience and seeing where your team stands at the end of the season. Sink back and soothe yourself in the sickly gloop of hearsay and wallow in the crackpot shallowness of it all.

There are scientists taking a break from explaining the universe in order to try and work out Rafa's latest formation. They'll soon head back to their laboratories: oh for the quiet life. If the Voronin plan was for him to go missing for long periods of the game and make it up as he went along, it worked perfectly. Quite why Reading are deemed worthy of two defensive midfielders, no one knows. It's a strategy that's never worked yet. Tell another supporter that the rumoured £20 million required for Mascherano's purchase might be a tad excessive and they go all Torquemada on you. Sometimes his passing is dreadful and he makes little or no creative contribution. The collapse of his move would only cause real concern because it'd trigger Rafa's next (final?) hissy fit. Whilst Sissoko should erase the word 'footballer' from any documentation in his possession before the fraud squad is tipped off. Did Juventus really offer us £12 million?

But both of them in the same team? Pundits who rarely praise Liverpool do give begrudging respect to our defence. To give it such protection and still concede three goals is the height of absurdity. Like a man who wears a belt and braces, Rafa doesn't even trust his own pants. Protecting Hobbs may have been a factor, but it was self-defeating and Agger can't return soon enough. We handed the initiative to the home side while we struggled with the new formation like an octopus with scotch tape at Christmas.

The penalty was harsh, but it was a poor challenge by Carragher anyway. Reading's home record is none too shabby, and we've made it even better. Our own record at 0-1 during Rafa's reign is appalling. All we've gained so far this season is the three points from that freak-show at Goodison Park. Whining about penalties conceded/not given makes us sound like Moyes and his gargoyle ilk over the way. On that comical day in October Gerrard was replaced on 70 minutes, the game still to be won, after allegedly playing without intelligence. A game in Europe was a few days later, coincidentally. He gave away a stupid free kick that handed Reading the lead again, and at 1-3 with 25 minutes to go he was replaced - with Marseille three days off. Premiership priority? I wish I had a laugh left.

We swapped centre-halves with ten minutes remaining. Even with everything he's achieved, Ferguson would get lynched if he did anything so crushingly negative or disinterested - and rightly so. They've had their blip at Bolton, followed by three easy home games to get back on track. We've got Marseille, United, Chelsea and Portsmouth.

I expect Rafa will moan to the FA about that too.

19th DECEMBER
Marseille 0 Liverpool 4 (11/12/07)
Liverpool 0 Man U 1 (16/12/07)

He's great, Euro-Rafa. Never doubted him for a second. But at the weekend Anglo-Rafa failed once more. Strap yourself in for the ride, it's about to get bumpy again. Last week's column contained a rare moment of innocence. Forecasting a smooth sail in choppy waters has drowned many a man. This is the way of things at this level. You want to be the best there is? The demands of millions of spoilt brats baying for your blood after the slightest mishap are compulsory.

To stay at Anfield, eschew foreign ownership, spend what we can afford and settle for whatever success comes our way may be the Puritan ethos of choice – but by God it would be dull. Liverpool is a name that reverberates longer and shines brighter than almost any other you care to mention. So the screeching melodrama that inevitably pursues anyone seated at the top table has to be tolerated, any Olde Worlde disgust for the Cirque Du Lunatique that stalks us suppressed.

Sometimes you can at least savour a performance like last

Tuesday's in France, but were the post-Reading doubters so wide of the mark? The team chosen was exactly what we've demanded throughout these rotational years: 4-4-2, everyone in chosen positions and purpose shown from the first whistle. Is it so difficult to do this every match? It's not about changing the odd player here or there, it's the grinding gears of questionable tactics; forcing dumb footballers to think; giving average opposition respect they don't deserve. Benayoun and Kewell out wide, not Voronin or Kuyt. A midfield with attacking power and defensive solidity. Forwards combining pace, work-rate and skill.

Next stop: rocket science. Rafa has everyone dancing to his tune. Pundits gave him credit for Gerrard's master-class (yes, that 20-minute rest at Reading made all the difference) but debated at 3-0 whether he should start resting players for United. There were still 40 minutes to go! Torres had one of his unstoppable days. The opposition was again maligned, as if being swept aside by Liverpool is irrefutable proof of ineptitude. Nobody ever confused me with a cheerleader – despite the short skirt and pom-poms – but sometimes all you can do is express admiration for an almost flawless performance.

But it's games like Reading or rather Rafa's approach to them that causes concern. We're not good enough to meddle, and the manager has too much ego not to. An exasperating conundrum. If the Yanks spent their goodwill in the face-off with Rafa, they've gone into the red with reports of a climb-down over the stadium. Such chatter appearing the day before United show up did not go unnoticed by conspiracy theorists, but it indicates how much they've been damaged by Tracksuit-gate that fans believe anything about them now. Apologists will rally in the face of financial mischief; "It won't be a £700 million loan, it's £400 million" – whoopity doo. For a second there I thought we were in trouble.

There are rumours Moores regrets selling now. I hope his conscience sticks needles in his guts at night, but cash was always the rancid soul's panacea. It's what most fans wanted though. The response has been Glazerian, the new owners no longer saviours but saboteurs. If you sell your soul don't feign surprise when you see the devil greasing up and licking his lips. Events on Sunday merely exacerbated the annoyance with the Reading result. United do so little to take the points nowadays I'm amazed Rafa doesn't forfeit them in lieu of a week's rest. Who knew we would ever pine for Houllier, when hiding behind our obvious inferiority meant blanket defence, surrendered possession and sneaky undeserved goals? It's bad enough the Mancs made our title their own, now they've swiped the one thing we had going for us in this decade, because that was barefaced larceny on Sunday.

Or was it? How galling is it that in the areas where our manager is supposed to be the master – discipline, organisation, strategy and airtight defence – we came off distinctly second best again. Every scuffed pass, every deflection, every bobble, it all went their way. I suspect witchcraft is involved, have done for the 30-odd years I've been watching this fixture.

I'll stop right there. A grown man crying is not a particularly edifying spectacle.

Christmas fortnight
Chelsea 2 Liverpool 0 (19/12/07)
Liverpool 4 Portsmouth 1 (22/12/07)
Derby 1 Liverpool 2 (26/12/07)
Man City 0 Liverpool 0 (30/12/07)

Lost to Chelsea, yawned, moved on. Now there's a sentence you thought you'd never read. One glance at the line-up demonstrated precisely where the Carling Cup lies in the Rafa-scheme. In the drinking pit I frequent on a far too regular basis I wondered why on earth 6,000 fellow Reds even bothered going down there. This hasn't always been the case. I once went to Burnley when we'd already clinched the tie in the first leg and had a great night. Distance and inconvenience were no object once upon a time. One game at Palace was postponed an hour before kick-off and I still went to the rearranged fixture. Football takes the piss so much nowadays, small acts of rebellion like last Wednesday's are all we have left. I'll be there for the league game in February, when it matters.

At least I hope it does. For this one I had my back to the screen for most of the night, the ooh's and aah's of everyone else making me turn around to see what happened. Let's just say I didn't have neck-ache when the evening mercifully ended. There were small stirrings of contempt once Lampard ahem 'scored' and wheeled away with a finger raised. Anyone else involved in such a fluke would have a semblance of dignity, smiled sheepishly and shrugged – but this is Chelsea, and class is something children sit in.

Not that we're any better sometimes. Peter Crouch may know what went on in that addled head of his when he ranted about foreign divers but nobody else does. Still, accusations of racism are a bit much. It's not an isolated instance either, as Chelsea used the race card against the Grant doubters in his managerial infancy. Like I say, classy. They could easily have mentioned the extraordinary coincidence of Gerrard going to ground much too easily at the precise moment his penalty technique improved. Or they could just show footage of any game involving Joe Cole and close the case there and then. Someone near me went ballistic after Shevchenko's strike. You really wonder about the English education system, when they can't even translate a team-sheet or calculate the quantum leap in Liverpudlian ennui. Or see Babel taken off and Voronin left out there, yet still think we endeavoured to rescue the situation. The thought of an all Merseyside semi-final was too hideous to contemplate, and lifting this cup wouldn't save Rafa anyway. Ask Houllier about 2003.

Portsmouth began a sequence of league games that we're more than capable of winning and took on far more significance than a trinket only Chelsea seem to covet. Why should Rafa rotate anyway, when the players seem perfectly capable of taking breathers in the middle of a game? Just as at Marseille a two-goal lead was the signal to surrender possession, impetus and desire. Surely when the boot is on the throat one lusty step forward is all that's required to end matters? Initially Pompey showed no inclination to take advantage of such charity, needing half-time and the explanations of their manager (presumably with the help of chalk and visual aids) that ten men behind the ball wasn't going to get them back in the game.

They almost scored immediately after the break, and then later they actually did. Thankfully our lads stepped up the necessary gear and made the game safe again, but it doesn't always work out that way. Having his God-like status tarnished somewhat by a prolonged spell in Rio Ferdinand's back pocket Torres was back to terrorising the plebeians of the Premiership. Short of watching a spotty yob throwing a pensioner's zimmer frame into a skip there can't have been a crueller sight than Fernando toying with Campbell like a cat with a half-dead bird. It was good to see Mascherano show signs of creativity at last. He certainly stepped up the pace of the game at 2-1, and did so without much assistance from a strangely subdued Gerrard. The usual casual dismissal of the result followed, but bullying the lower orders is fine by me. It's the next evolutionary step up from last season and results like Reading are still stuck in the craw.

Had we, as looked likely at one stage, drawn at Derby County there may already be idle chatter about the next Liverpool manager. If they'd scored their other chance at 1-1 before Gerrard (more gleefully than was dignified) took his it may well have been a lot more than gossip.

Perhaps our leader had heard the same moronic anti-Scouse bilge pouring from the home sections that we did. I don't know what it is about these places but they go missing from the top flight for years and come back on a mission to nauseate. You hear the odd stupid thing at every ground, and it's not like my skin is wafer-thin any more, but this was way, way over the top.

It was a delicious irony to 'steal' all three points right at the end of a game we had struggled to get to grips with, this despite an early advantage from the obligatory Torres magic. It all seemed far too easy and we could see it getting away from the players long before the equaliser. All's well that ends, as they say.

The trip to City was unusual in that we may as well have been the home team. Sven has been praised to the skies by City fans thus far, but one wonders if even this point didn't come at a psychic cost. For ourselves we huffed and puffed again, reminiscent of those dark days when Houllier would count the shots and pretend that statistic counted for anything. A lot were from distance and a lot flew wide. Rafa counted them as "chances" anyway and claimed all was well.

It wasn't.

Chapter 6

January

5th JANUARY

Halfway assessment

In the summertime we dreamt of 80 points and whether it would be enough to finish top. Now that auld acquaintance be forgot for another year we realise it won't suffice. Despite starting badly and without hitting top gear United are on course for another 90. We probably won't even meet our own 'realistic' target and doubts still remain.

Our record against the 'other' three is still pitiful, and it's only Chelsea's numerous difficulties and Arsenal's relative inexperience keeping us within spitting distance and still to visit all three. Then there are the infuriating caprices of our troubled, troubling manager. He got his money, and he still wasn't happy. Tracksuit-Gate was a sly manipulation of public sentiment. If his players could pass the ball like he passes the buck history would be rewritten. The Brazil side of 1970 would be a footnote renowned merely for their caveman ways in comparison. Whether it was Heinze, TV schedules, the fixture list, international breaks, Gerrard's toe or those meddlesome know-nothings in the US of A (you know, his employers!) he gave a sterling performance of a man producing miracles in the face of insurmountable odds. Maybe we won't win the league in spring, but an Oscar could be on the cards.

We'll find out what Hicks and Gillett are really up to with our club soon enough. In the short-term it's irrelevant to what's happening on the pitch. Ask our Mancunian friends, peering down at us from on high, what they think of Glazer and watch those cherubic visages turn a fetching shade of vein-streaked puce. The soul of LFC was whored out to the highest bidder and will never be returned to us. It will slip through one sweaty grasp after another. We could at least watch a decent team to make that barbaric act of treachery remotely palatable.

It's pointless arguing about the precise amount they gave the manager from their own pocket. Abramovich bulldozed the landscape to such an extent that fans forgot how these things ought to work. Rafa got £45 million's worth of new players plus another year out of Mascherano whatever his eventual destination. To secure such riches he merely sold players who'd made little contribution to last season's 68 points and Champions League final anyway. A significant improvement on that record is vital or he is sadly no better than anyone else. It is a cause for mild bewilderment that he is 'technically' still on course to achieve that.

Benitez may think he was clever in shifting responsibility for our occasional stutters onto the Yanks but they won't forgive or forget in a hurry, even if he has hoodwinked too many supporters. His obsession with rotation and fitness will be the death of his and our ambitions. He has thankfully realised that if you have remarkable talents like Torres and Gerrard they must play as often as humanly possible, but there are still times he underestimates the opposition and lands in hot water. Such occasions can be easily identified when reports invoke the term Voronin, Ukrainian for 'barrel bottom'.

This carelessness was most evident in Europe, where the later miracles wouldn't have been necessary had precautions been taken earlier in the group. In August I was asking for the level two teams in England to step up, not only to give Liverpool the kick up the arse they needed but also to take precious points from our rivals. Worryingly, Everton and City have taken this request much too literally and their halitosis breath is tickling our neck hairs to an alarming degree. It's been a strange season all told. Some more wins and we might even have ourselves an actual title challenge at long last. Drop more points (the visits to Reading and Derby indicate this is the more likely scenario) and we'll pray for The Miracle Of Moscow to make the season bearable.

And check next summer's managerial shortlist before babbling about Transition yet again. You have been warned.

9th JANUARY

Liverpool 1 Wigan 1 (02/01/08)

Luton Town 1 Liverpool 1 (06/01/08)

I'm rarely lost for words. Ask anyone who knows me, I can babble like a short-changed Thai hooker with a stutter, yet I sat quietly shivering throughout the Wigan game with one solitary thought echoing round my head: what's he up to now? One up front and five in midfield at home to a team facing relegation. Fans who were ready to string up Sven by his overused gonads for applying that strategy to us were shamed into silence. So not all bad news then.

It's been a good week for hush. Having read Ferguson's preposterous lecture to the Manc masses, it was as if we weren't letting United outshine us. We can be just as quiet as you lot. Quieter! The long-awaited 'singing section' in the Kop hasn't worked. They just get on with it and everybody ignores them. It doesn't help when they sing 15-minute dirges for a manager that's starting to seriously irritate everyone. He's knocking on the gate isn't he? They're getting ready to welcome him into Liverpool Manager Heaven, where he'll swap tales of what might have been with Roy and Gerard. Not Souness of course, he's in the other place.

Last Wednesday saw a contest between fans and players, all grappling with the manager's convoluted game plan. The result ironically was a draw. No one understood. Watching this team trying to unlock packed defences is to witness panic in its purest form. As a randy teenager I unhooked bras with more finesse.

There was a forlorn hope the wingers were supposed to get behind Wigan, but sadly an unfit Pennant and a slothful Kewell (does he finally realise there's no new contract coming?) weren't up to the job.

Steve Bruce has the evil eye on Rafa, wonky as it is. He'd not lost a league game to him during his Birmingham stint either. It's hardly a brainwave. Stay back, run around a lot and kick as much as the referee allows. With Steve Bennett, that meant a lot – with the added bonus of Liverpool players being penalised for every stupid thing. None of which matters if our team struggles to help itself. It was so curiously tame and distant. Few in the crowd wanted to be there, knowing there would be precious little excitement to save us from plummeting temperatures. Titus Bramble got his long-awaited revenge. He's been cheered onto the pitch by Kopites before now, such was his ability to create mayhem within his own ranks, but he's had the last laugh and you can't reasonably begrudge him a second of it.

So all that money on players and an extended loan for Mascherano in order to extend our title hopes to the second day of the New Year? Bargain! They really should release Rafa's next plea for funds on DVD and file it under Comedy Classics. Given how strapped for cash we're supposed to be Luton had a nerve asking for our half of Sunday's gate receipts. I've hated them since the 80's, thanks to the plastic pitch, an away fan ban and their townsfolk's predilection for electing far-right MP's. Once they lost their unfair advantages they sank down the leagues and no one shed a tear. If we've money to throw away use it for our own. The legendary Ray Kennedy suffers from Parkinson's Disease and needs all the help he can get. Some fans are organising numerous benefits and donations for the great man; I'll return to the subject in future columns, rest assured.

In the end it was just a crass media hatchet job to fashion a 'grudge' match from meagre materials. Win and we're the robber barons. Lose or draw and Luton get their money anyway so we're the upper-class twits who got what was coming. Liverpool have a dreadful record of PR incompetence but for once they simply had nowhere to go. Stitched up, in short. Besides, Luton could always get that bung money back off the agents. They fought hard to be fair but with confidence around our ankles we're easy pickings for anyone lately. Where does Kuyt find the self-respect to get out of bed? Another fistful of changes and the apologista still expect cohesion. When are you going to see the blatantly obvious fact staring you in the face?

This manager won't change his ways. There's an irony there if you look hard enough. I've long since passed the point of caring.

16th JANUARY
Middlesbrough 1 Liverpool 1 (12/01/08)

Wake me up when Inter are in town. They're my words incidentally, not a quote from a player though your confusion would be understandable. Why should this season be any different from the others? The writing's on the wall and it'll take more than a bit of whitewash to camouflage it.

The title race is getting tense. It includes a Chelsea side seemingly damaged beyond repair by injury, internationals, regime change and infighting. Sadly it no longer includes us. The last fragment of hope was atomised in a bleak northern wasteland. How fitting. We're like one of those 10,000 metre runners who shuffle pitifully into lane three while the leaders lap them with boundless vitality. Let the internal backbiting and bickering commence as the last veneer of defiance is erased by a twin onslaught of logic and history.

Names of potential replacements will be snorted in derision. I've seen it all as a veteran of the Souness, Evans and Houllier Wars. I'll sit this one out, because this has the potential to be the nastiest yet judging by the opening skirmishes. Of course the names being 'short-listed' aren't inspiring. They never are. Somewhere however a coach is doing sterling work and doesn't even realise he is unhappy in his current position. Then the name 'Liverpool' will be mentioned and he'll suddenly find all sorts of things wrong within his club that he'd never noticed before. Ask Rafa, he knows how it works.

It was absolutely hilarious how Klinsmann became all things to all men. For those eager to mock the Yanks' wispy knowledge of 'soccer' being linked with such a part-timer was definitive proof that the new owners were not fit for purpose. It was no use reminding people that Bayern are run by great football men like Hoeness and Beckenbauer so maybe Hicks & Gillett know something after all – although making our bid public is the act of a coward and has only made matters worse. For those bored with Rafa's Controlball, news of one of the game's great strikers getting the job saw a few eyebrows raised in intrigue, and of course the press had a field day. The rumours undermined Benitez, turned a schism into a chasm and when Jurgen naturally chose the biggest club in his homeland they danced with delight at such incontrovertible 'proof' of Liverpool's molecular place in the scheme of things.

Greater evidence of our exclusion from the elite came from the actual football. After Benitez practically declared war on his employers we gave Newcastle a football lesson. We scored three. On Saturday night the Geordies went back to school, but the Mancs got six goals to prove beyond doubt they were infinitely better than their opponents. Our finishing has been poor for years. It was ironic that our most destructive weapon, Torres, was the main reason we didn't spank Newcastle in November, but recently the rest couldn't hit a cow's arse with a banjo. The players don't seem bothered, with one or two notable exceptions. It's as if they know the need to impress this particular manager has more or less been vaporised. They'll claim catching his eye was pointless anyway, as great performances never guarantee you a front-row seat in Rafa's rotational hell.

Those who intuitively clutch at straws noted we'd scored our first goal in Middlesbrough for six years (a cracker it was too) and that Arsenal lost there "so they're no mugs, lad". Spare us. When the Dependables, like Reina and Arbeloa, are suddenly putting in nervous and error-strewn performances something is going wrong. Torres and Gerrard were meant to be the jewels in a long-awaited crown. They're turning into eye-catching wallpaper plastered over widening cracks. Swap Owen for Torres and it could be 2004 all over again. That Voronin is ever given a shirt ahead of Crouch shows this manager to be as petty as his predecessor, and only a miracle can save him from a similar fate.

We tried to convince everyone of our higher calling, but are finally back in the pack where we belong. It's a pack of managers helping their clubs punch above their weight – bar one. Such a concept is now totally alien to swathes of Liverpool's support who cannot talk about anything but money any more.

That clinking clanking sound will ultimately be the death of us all.

23rd JANUARY
Liverpool 5 Luton Town 0 (15/01/08)
Liverpool 2 Aston Villa 2 (21/01/08)

Greetings from Comedy Central. As outsiders clutch their aching sides we witty Scousers keep delivering the goods. They're rolling in the aisles of London and Manchester anyway. Where will it end? Hicks denies wanting to sell up. Bush's bosom buddy has a similar same stubborn streak. He won't retreat despite the hysterical chaos he helped create. Iraq, Anfield, it's all the same to them.

Dubai is now revered as a potential liberator from the Americans! That's how I like my irony, friends. The fact they dragged their feet so lethargically last year is a distant, inconvenient memory. There were even hints about another march before Monday, which would have made three in eight months. We may be hurting inside but at least we're getting some exercise. Beneath the layers of weirdness lies the oddest fact of all; Benitez – currently 14 points behind the leaders – is apparently the indisputable keeper of the Anfield flame, protector in chief of The Liverpool Way. That's right. The man who played one up front at home to Wigan and replaced his best players when losing to Reading. Who, sarcastically maybe, touted for the England job in a Liverpool press conference and gave 20 different questions the same answer in a fit of pique. Who is linked to managerial posts abroad at precisely such times he demands yet more transfer money.

The coincidences keep coming. Several papers claimed Rafa keeps his job if D.I.C. conquer The Great Satan. An alarming number of supporters think the manager is acting on our behalf with selfless zeal. There is even talk of empires crumbling if Rafa leaves, from fans who witnessed the departures of Shankly, Keegan, Paisley, Souness, Rush and Dalglish and who struggled with the traumas of Heysel and Hillsborough. But if we lost the manager who hasn't summoned one realistic title bid – even Evans managed two – we are to be naught but dust. Mention events in November, ask who threw the snowball that created the avalanche and you're lashed with obscenity that would make a sailor blush.

If anyone should think me supportive of the bloated cowboy and his immorally silent partner, please leave the adults to talk and go play with your crayons. Once 'we' auctioned the soul of this formerly proud institution it was only a matter of time before we were passed around like the after-dinner mints. Spurious tales of ocean-deep transfer kitties hypnotised the masses. Their greed, gullibility and ignorance of how LFC became what it is fuelled this ghastly farce and the inevitable duplicity has only increased the ferocity of the subsequent backlash. It's painful to hear supporters now kid themselves about the Arabs' future generosity. Whatever happened to "once bitten"? If Dubai gets control by spending more than originally planned and commits to the white elephant stadium, the manager's transfer kitty shrinks further. Benitez won't hang around for that, thus betraying those that howl in his defence. I could laugh, but gallows humour tends to hurt the neck.

Villa was the sort of performance we've seen too often lately.

The lack of a killer instinct haunts us. In our finest Premiership season 77 of those 82 points came from the 27 games in which we scored first. Fat lot of good it's doing us now. Bullying a depleted Luton is one thing, beating a tough Premiership outfit that dares stand up to us another. Did the visitors even do that much? Not really, but a little goes an awfully long way at Anfield nowadays.

Check the stats; if the club were to fine players each time they missed the target we could buy out the Americans and still have change to irrigate Africa. There are some you can rely on, but Gerrard and Torres can't save our arses all the time. And can anyone explain why Crouch is being treated the way he is? It defies belief, but everyone has retreated to the trenches while logic is blown to smithereens in no-man's land. Hicks will be blamed for absolutely everything now whilst the fans' eternal lament cries out; "Give Rafa everything he needs to complete the job."

Personally I don't think there's enough money in the world, but just lately I seem to be in a very small minority.

30th JANUARY
Liverpool 5 Havant 2 (26/01/08)

So what happens now? We sang some songs, and rather inconveniently the buggers still won't budge. Shouldn't they have surrendered by now? It wasn't my idea to have my photograph published. I don't really want to be identified as the foul-mouthed red-faced lunatic hurling abuse at the manager when Crouch came on against Villa in the 80th minute. A little anonymity, please. It shows how much faith I've lost in the guy that the tirade merely increased after the equaliser. The salvaging of a point might have meant some praise was due but I wearily confess I've gone beyond the point of fairness.

During the eventful cup-tie at the weekend there were times when Liverpool fans turned on each other and it's sad to see. I love my city and feel a certain pride in the fact there is no

Goliath we won't fight, but sooner or later we'll have to recognise the situation we're in. We may clamber out of the frying pan even yet but it will be no cooler should D.I.C. gain control. People are disappointed and it's understandable. Up to a point. An unpleasant experience it may be but put yourselves in Hicks' shoes. In their shocking naivety what have many Liverpool supporters demanded? Money to buy out the previous 'owners'; a huge transfer slush fund for a manager who can't even summon a title challenge; a shiny new stadium. We're talking in excess of one billion dollars (feel free to impersonate Dr Evil). Oh, one more thing – don't put any debt on the club itself. And if you could get around to curing cancer in the next five minutes, that would be just peachy.

If Hicks wore a purple coat and top hat, twirled a cane and sang a few bars of 'Pure Imagination' the situation could not be any more fantastical, even if the Kop calls him something that only sounds like Wonka. So let's settle down a little bit and realise what has happened. Last year a decision was taken on our behalf that changed Liverpool FC forever. No one should blame Moores for this, despite his dubious and doubtless coincidental decision to sell to those who offered him more money. He and Parry had been screeched at for years about finding 'investment'. Yet in the Dictionary Of The Gullible that word has now come to mean 'massive, string-free handout'. We're talking about two American billionaires here. Dallas wasn't fiction; it was a documentary!

Many people over here in England read the column too and I received a few e-mails refuting that I was in a small minority regarding Benitez. We're getting to be like a secret society, because dissent to the majority view provokes a Tasmanian Devilish response. A poll in the local press suggested the manager had a 94% approval rating, which frankly is baffling. Then you think about the damage caused by the Klinsmann episode, and wonder how a secret meeting got into the public domain. Rafa's been martyred while still alive – a neat trick.

Had it stayed 1-2 on Saturday he may not have had to wait much longer. Some people take these things far too seriously. We've often struggled against minnows; on one particularly nightmarish night in the Souness era we trailed 3-0 to Chesterfield. But this was Havant & Waterlooville with their collection of bricklayers and bin men, their dreadful joke-friendly name lying 120 places below ours. The newspapers had a field day, gloating and punning with equal vigour, and even the predictable outcome couldn't change things. This was the definition of a no-win situation. There's no point getting irritated, it's like arguing with children. The very fact you're doing it reflects poorly on your own character.

The romance of the cup? Whatever. Our sheer awfulness at times beggared belief. There may have been worse debuts than Skrtel's but I have thankfully scraped them off my memory circuits. One headline beforehand read "Liverpool were left reeling by news of Voronin's injury", written by somebody whose comedy genius is yet to be appreciated by the rest of the world. Benayoun up front had a nice look to it, so some good may come of Saturday. The dispute with the Americans will drag on and we Havant a clue what happens next.

See what I did there?

Chapter 7

February

6th FEBRUARY

West Ham 1 Liverpool 0 (30/01/08)

Liverpool 3 Sunderland 0 (02/02/08)

Look out Mancs we're gaining on ya! Well, technically. Wouldn't it be nice to read about the football occasionally? Sadly we've gone beyond the point of no return on that front. Hicks may be a pernicious carpetbagger but it's lucky for some that he's such a comically demonic hate figure because too many are hiding behind him now. He's a shark and acts exactly the way you'd expect; swimming around, sniffing for blood. Moores, Parry and Gillett – and thus our football club – were absolutely drenched in the stuff, or is that just in my murderously feverish imagination?

It's amazing the easy ride those three are getting. Moores sold the club to someone who couldn't afford it; Parry was so conscious of fan protests that he turns up in a brand new Ferrari in solidarity. Gillett's silence has convinced some fans he's an avuncular scatterbrain duped like the rest of us. Supporters aren't entirely exempt from criticism either. A lot of outrage has been fuelled by a collective guilt for not protesting a year ago and swallowing whole Parry's "Trust us" bullshit instead of laughing him out of town. Even now we're meant to believe Moores is fighting our battles behind closed doors and Gillett is our best hope for a deal with the saintly, stain-free Dubai. Anyone believing any of that quite frankly deserves every shafting they get, past present or future.

As for the proposed buy-out by 100,000 supporters I have to be careful what I say. I know Rogan Taylor quite well and he's always been equal parts fascinating and infuriating, and I've no wish to pour cold water on ambitious schemes especially when they come from the heart, but the cynic in me always wins out in the end. As stated previously I love our quixotic stand-offs with windmills but now it's becoming farcical. If it were a realistic proposal it might even strengthen Hicks' hand by giving him someone to play off against Dubai, who must surely be sick of the whole fiasco.

I don't know why I'm getting worked up about it. I haven't got five grand anyway and wouldn't pay if I had. This is nothing but financial and emotional blackmail, handing huge profit to a slimy pair of cut-throats. While the thought of Moores counting his blood money and crying crocodile tears will give me an aneurysm if I'm not careful. So much for wanting to write about the games!

Sunderland saw a return to winning ways, but West Ham sent a shudder through the ranks that still hasn't subsided. Whatever your thoughts about any blame that can be apportioned to the fiscal disarray, sympathy ebbs away when Kuyt's sweat is continually preferred to Crouch's threat. If only Rafa would show a sign of wanting to help himself. It was bitterly ironic to see his team punished for throwing too many players forward, but that's the kind of misfortune that plagues strugglers. We finally got to see Torres & Crouch together on Saturday, and after an hour there was already an understanding developing between the two and a few goals. Rafa has to try and make this work, or the meagre support he may have will simply evaporate. Mascherano's willingness to chase lost causes got the fans going, along with Pennant's persistence (despite his sporadic accuracy). Carragher of all people had to show him how it's done, just in case anyone thought things weren't weird enough in L4. Bootle's finest has struggled of late but his goalkeeping remains impeccable.

Keane certainly thought Styles' summer spanking influenced events, but the refereeing in all Big 4 matches is highly suspect nowadays. Fear has definitely crippled officials, emphasised by Ferguson's predictable bile despite a shocking Nani tackle, Evra's handball and Rooney's incessant backchat at the weekend. Referees have their careers to think of, don't you know.

A small but fervent band of Reds stayed behind to protest about the Americans. It's the same fans who sing throughout, hand out leaflets, stage meetings, get things organised, while the rest of the Kop filed out almost before the final whistle. FC United was greeted with a degree of disdain in these parts, but a significant portion of our support is so alienated, angry and disenfranchised that surely a Scouse equivalent cannot be far away?

13th FEBRUARY
Chelsea 0 Liverpool 0 (10/02/08)

Liverpool fans may have numerous vociferous critics but it's safe to say Rafa isn't one of them. He's constantly kissing our backsides in the press, not an entirely unpleasant experience. There are a few cynical toads casting doubt on these odes to our magnificence because they became far more frequent once his spat with Hicks went public, but what can you do with such spiritual chaff except pity them for their meanness?

He's also started bellyaching about internationals again, convinced we're the only ones to suffer. He's complained from day one of the season in truth, one thing that can't be blamed on the Yanks. I'm sure the Rafapologista will give it a damn good go, anyway. Once Torres limped out of Spain's game earplugs became compulsory headwear in the Melwood press ranks. Since he'd bizarrely claimed Crouch should be first choice for England (but not us) and given a spirited defence of Kuyt even before Fernando's misfortune it let him off the hook at the Bridge. God forbid he should have to pick his best two goal scorers again and prove everyone else right.

Events at Old Trafford for the 50th anniversary of Munich conspired to bring an ounce of credibility to my bumptious claim of gaining on the leaders. At this rate we'll reel them in by Christmas. That wasn't as bizarre as the week-long attempt to make United the arbiters of good taste within football grounds. I felt sorry for City as they were subtly and unpleasantly needled for days. In the end the only danger of disruption to such a moving occasion was the sigh of disappointment from those home fans eager to have their prejudices fuelled further. Still I'm sure the sound of sky blue (and Scouse) bones crackling on that bonfire they're always banging on about provided some small comfort. In an age of 'Grand Slam' Sundays no one can convince me this fixture couldn't have been avoided. Think back to the death of George Best, when City and Liverpool were not sanctioned for a minute's applause, and wonder. One paper even tried to blame the sound of distant fireworks on Liverpool supporters!

As often happens, various claims that they would 'put on a show' for the Babes' memory came to naught. Roy Evans once mentioned the 96 before an April match and was rewarded with an atrocious performance that seemed much worse for his evocation of loss. Should United reach another European final I fear it will again become lachrymose beyond belief, making their jibes against Liverpudlians doubly offensive.

But we had our own problems to overcome, not the least City overtaking us! Watching Chelsea get by without Terry, Drogba and Shevchenko left a bad taste in the mouth as Abramovich is the unwitting architect of our current malaise. With United's wealth rocketing skywards Liverpool were already hot to trot with anyone willing to part with their loot and fully prepared to ignore any flecks of blood on it. One Russian's helicopter ride over West London simply tipped us over the edge and possibly past the point of no return. It has not been the most edifying spectacle.

Watching both teams slug it out like two drunks on a bouncy

castle you would be hard pressed to gauge whose outlay was most wasteful. I heard The Liquidator on the radio the night before and, plagued forever by this superstitious monkey on my back, automatically assumed we'd lose. Without Torres and lucky to get the nil in seven previous visits one didn't need psychic powers to guess we wouldn't score – but Chelsea's caution wasn't a shock either. The greatest league in the world? Let's hope Scudamore and his grasping gringos aren't proposing to show this match to the slathering masses of the world. The poor bastards in Guantanamo Bay wouldn't want to watch this muck.

The Reds seemed pleased with the point. When you've been punched in the mouth so often a slap on the cheek feels like a kiss. All we needed was someone, anyone, to put the ball in the net but I guess Cheyroux don't grow on trees. Rafa's taken eight teams to Chelsea and not one has scored. Maybe there's another club with a similarly atrocious record at any of the great cathedrals of football (or Stamford Bridge for that matter) but their name does not spring readily to mind.

The manager stomped around the technical area all afternoon. He did not seem a happy bunny. Imagine what he'd have been like if he'd paid to watch it.

20th FEBRUARY
Liverpool 1 Barnsley 2 (16/02/08)

Everyone at Liverpool will be in the dock soon. The charge? Perpetrating the biggest fraud since Salif Diao wrote "Occupation: Footballer" on his tax return.

They're all in on it. The manager, the players, the life president, the chief executive – even the fans. If it weren't for the legal and financial might of Dubai, prosecutors would probably be trying to drag the sheikh in too as a co-conspirator. It's an extremely elaborate hoax, fashioned late last year in a smoky dark room in the furthest recesses of Anfield. Its purpose: to separate two Americans from their goldmine.

It is in fact an intriguing twist on an old con; usually dumb colonials are fooled into paying huge amounts for something that's actually worthless. Remember the gimp who bought London Bridge, thinking it was Tower Bridge? Think about it. We'd sold the club to the wrong people, that much was obvious. So how to get it back? Simple; make them think they've bought the wrong club.

Poor football. A manager out of his depth. Greedy, disinterested players. Weekly demonstrations of fan discontent. Embarrassing results against lower opposition. Tabloid manna from heaven, and no trophies. It's crystal clear; we're trying to trick Hicks and Gillett into thinking they've bought Newcastle. It's so obvious I feel stupid for not having spotted it before. It might have saved me two months of mania and heartache. How could I have ever doubted them? Our finishing couldn't be that bad. We couldn't possibly be this disjointed under the most methodical manager of the era. We would never have a rotation policy that makes you think a blindfold and pin is somehow involved. We wouldn't allow Titus Bramble to score at Anfield to help Wigan get a point. Two goals in three minutes for Villa, a draw at Luton, a non-league team in the lead at Anfield (twice), a championship side with an atrocious away record coming from behind to knock us out of the cup. It's just not possible.

Remember Carragher's uncharacteristic lunges that gave away crucial penalties at Reading and West Ham? When it begins to look a shade too obvious we throw them off the scent. Even those idiots would have caught on if we'd not beaten Derby County, but we left it late for added drama and made it look like a fluke. I only hope Saturday wasn't too blatant. Losing to Barnsley might tip off even the dimmest billionaire.

It's really the manager who deserves the bravos and encores. It's been an astonishing portrayal of a man drowning in his own vacuity; babbling about controlling games and missed chances, with a side-order dollop of glutinous sentiment for the wonderful, wonderful fans as a bonus. Rafa really should do King Lear one day. We've done our bit too don't forget. Protesting, marching, on-line petitioning, booing the final whistle, staying behind after games to howl our disapproval, whining to anyone with a TV camera. We've drawn the line at exposing our big fat guts to the elements and leaving huge empty spaces in the stands with minutes to go like the Geordies do. You don't want to overplay your hand. I especially enjoyed the way we made Barnsley's keeper look a world-beater. Every shot was tricky but not impossible to stop, while at the other end Itandje's portrayal of a blundering buffoon could mean a late Oscar entry

Handing Kuyt the goal after months of nothing was a subtle touch that made it look like we meant business. Hyypia tried to give them the late penalty but we forgot referees are ingrained into giving nothing against the big four. A slight glitch in the plan, but we allowed them a free shot on the area's edge and all resolved itself. This elaborate plot is almost played out. With our club rapidly turning into a catastrophic mess, not worth a big fat zero to anyone, the Americans will as they say 'haul ass' soon enough, begging the Arabs to take this ramshackle, crumbling edifice off their grubby tremulous hands.

Once we're saved, what a transformation you will see then. The passing inch-perfect, shots flying into top corners, the best 11 players appearing all the time and leaving the field dripping with sweat after 90 minutes of ferocious endeavour, cheered to the rafters. Minnows swatted aside with consummate ease while United and co will be battered to a twitching pulp instead of being meekly offered the points. Get your money on the Reds for the grand slam of 2009. It's the safest bet in town.

Trust me.

27th FEBRUARY
Liverpool 2 Inter Milan 0 (19/02/08)
Liverpool 3 Middlesbrough 2 (23/02/08)

They're not fooling us for a minute. Beating Inter just sets us up for the mother of all falls. The blueprint to make Hicks think he's bought a dud remains unaltered. It took a while to decipher the stratagem and I'm reluctant to discredit the conspiracy theory after this reddest of herrings. Even his son's taking a slap now!

Few fans ever doubted the manager's ability on the European stage and it was hard not to sympathise with him last week. Win, and it 'proved' he was more concerned with Champions League glitter than he ever could be by domestic drudgery. Lose, and our season's over. He'd have to pack his bags to avoid further embarrassment by staining the kind of CV most European clubs still envy. Focus and commitment were total, and not just on the pitch. These are such great occasions, and you do begin to wonder who the fans are trying to kid when they claim the league must be the priority. Or do they pick up signals from the manager and the team then acts accordingly? Chicken or egg, which came first? Either way they both taste fowl (I am so, so sorry). Put another way; Shankly's bread and butter can't seem to compete with succulent foreign delicacies.

When we scored against Sunderland I stood to politely applaud. When Gerrard's late strike crept in the corner I flew three rows down in an almost orgiastic embrace with a total stranger, flattening anyone stupid enough to stray into our path. The result was casually, inevitably dismissed by the press corps, the scent of Rafa's blood in their nostrils clouding their judgement. One former Benitez acolyte even described the win as "smash and grab" – a frankly moronic assessment of events that even notorious Rafa-baiters in the redtops balked at.

Materazzi's dismissal had its effect and only the chauvinistic would deny it, but he was already finding Torres too hot to handle. It's not often our players can teach the great Zidane anything: Don't get mad, get even. Whether the Italian carthorse (once a blue, always a blue) was up to his usual whispering tricks, no one will ever know. Does Torres even have a sister to swap shirts with? The jaded still found cause for complaint. Our crossing and set pieces were all terrible. Gerrard's goal was exceptional, but you sensed he only chanced his arm because another centre would have failed abysmally to reach its target. All of this stuff can be improved on the training ground surely – so why is it getting worse? Where else does practise make imperfect?

Middlesbrough arrived and enthusiasm waned, rampant players replaced by sluggish lookalikes and vein-popping fans supplanted by soporific clones. As much as it would impact on the coffers the battle for fourth place just doesn't get the pulses racing. There is a significant reduction in the quality and importance of most Premiership clubs. Identikit dullards you couldn't pick out of a line-up, even if you'd watched them slap your granny with a sock full of sludge. This year's seen improvement in the traditionally bigger clubs, and surely Spurs will challenge next season too. The rest are interchangeable, to the point where relegating the bottom eight would barely register.

Things livened up when we fell behind, but I find bitching about offside beneath contempt. It's a stupid rule and ought to have been discarded years ago. The fabulous Torres put us in charge. Would you say despite being solo up front or because of it? We know what Rafa thinks because of his Valencia days. The team switched off again and the crowd went into hibernation assuming the worst was over, instinctively knowing how the rest of the game would pan out. One does not of course like to stereotype but a panicky last ten minutes was averted by Mascherano's Argentine tendencies fooling another generous referee and reducing Boro to ten men. Our luck appears to be in for once. He's become a crowd favourite through sheer bullishness, and would that more were like him.

Viewed in isolation this was as good a week as the previous one was damaging, but it will take a lot more to suppress dissent for manager or owners.

Chapter 8

March

5th MARCH

Bolton 1 Liverpool 3 (02/03/08)

Can things get any weirder? It's Liverpool 2008; of course they can. The previous situation wasn't ideal but at least you knew where you stood. Benitez or Hicks. Pick a side, no middle ground and no conscientious objectors. A fight to the death, we were told. So what are we supposed to make of the manager's newly discovered camaraderie with his nemesis?

Look, I don't like being cynical I really don't but the idea of Hicks sending 'supportive' e-mails to Rafa is bizarre. It will be interesting to see how the club's various rebel factions take this news, especially as it comes at a time when the Texan's position was beginning to wobble slightly. His son's reception in Anfield's most famous drinking establishment (think Christians and lions) could scarcely be misinterpreted as 'high spirits' while claiming Gillett couldn't sell to Dubai without his approval sounded like sabre-rattling, an emptying vessel making the most sound. So if Rafa finally had the enemy on the ropes what's with the public bonhomie? What does he know that we don't? Remember it was his original flounce that lit the blue touch paper for everything that's happened since.

Also, why tell people he doesn't speak to either Gillett or his son who have both seemingly vanished off the face of the earth? One newspaper claimed it was Gillett who initially approached Klinsmann and that his partner was 'only' guilty of a misguided public confession. "Aw shucks, I sure is sorreeee."

The popular Mascherano is finally signed and sealed, taking our so-called inadequate spending to around £70 million in less than a year. Form is returning gradually (Barnsley? Never heard of them) and the manager, previously thought to be dead meat on a hook, now sounds quietly content. Are we all really that shallow? Or is it just that in the wacky world of LFC anything can be reported and almost everything believed?

Gerrard gave the 'not good enough' speech that's been dusted off and recycled for most of the last 18 years. The tough-but-honest, heartfelt appraisal delivered in the hope of convincing the "patrons" (yet another PR faux pas from the Beverly Hillbillies) that the players are hurting just as much as we are. I recall similar eulogies from Jamie Redknapp in the 90's. The faces change but the platitudes linger on. Needless to say this was twisted into open warfare between captain and manager. "The one man Benitez cannot take on", wrote one inky reptile. Carragher's said virtually the same thing before and no one blinked, but a story linking him to a move would spin twice and then lie embarrassingly flat on the ground. To complete the circle of deceit, up pops the obligatory hijack bid from Real Madrid – for the manager and the captain this time. One day I'll keep all the cuttings in a folder and cross-reference; I'm sure they're all recycled word for word.

The comfortable win at Bolton proved we're serious about fourth spot. Which is reassuring, since Everton and Villa are no flash in the pan. The challenge is real. For years a seat on the gravy train has been reserved for us, third or fourth class usually. Everyone conveniently stepped aside to let us through no matter how poor we were. It helps recently that the luck has changed. Red cards here, misplaced back passes there. A keeper deflecting a shot in with his face is a new one on me though.

There was something missing on Sunday. Bolton complain as much, dive as much, base their game plan on set pieces as per – but it lacked the sprinkling of spite we've come to expect. Allardyce took his poisonous attitude toward Benitez with him, and this no longer felt like a grudge match. Torres played like Rafa had frightened him beforehand. He clearly expected to be set upon, and never got it together once he realised he'd been spared the worst. Blood usually spills at this most soulless of bowls. He wasn't needed in the end. Babel threatened often, which hasn't always been the case when he's started. It felt like the earlier away games, when a lead was the catalyst for swift intelligent counterattack, the likes of which we've rarely seen since.

Maybe we're going to finish like we started. In this most unstable of seasons, expect the unexpected.

12th MARCH
Liverpool 4 West Ham 0 (05/03/08)
Liverpool 3 Newcastle 0 (08/03/08)

It's not often I'm grateful for all the grisly machinations behind the scenes, but at least I get to write about something interesting. A winning team is boring. Yeah right, boo hoo – good football and a stronger league position. Life is hellish.

But recent games have followed a familiar pattern; early luck, goal from Torres, goal from Gerrard, frustrating period of opposition keep-ball, final flurry, three points. It's becoming awkward for those of us who doubted the manager. He could well prevent the thread his job hung by from finally snapping. The Rafapologista are getting cockier now. It's not worth wasting the energy needed to remind them how appalling the opposition has been of late because no one will be listening. And fair enough I say. It's been a long, occasionally excruciating, season and if you can't revel in a few wins after what we've had to put up with then you shouldn't be a Red full stop. Even if hammering the Hammers and slapping the car-Toon Army silly does have the feel of stepping on an ant with rickets.

There are games coming up that will test Liverpool's rediscovered resolve, but bridges can't be crossed before you come to them. A win and some priceless comedy from our ex-treble-chasing chums above us – you don't often get days like those. Last Wednesday wasn't bad either. Given the night off Euro-duty because of a double booking with Arsenal at the San Siro, it was the Hammers' turn to submit to the genius of Torres. Who cares if he rarely displays his inestimable gifts 'on the road'? Anfield is as good a place of worship as any and he's been nigh on unstoppable there. When you list the names of those Liverpool legends that never scored three in successive home games, it makes you wonder if Torres can take his place in the pantheon. Has there been a louder ovation than the one that greeted his substitution? Maybe when Kenny returned days before the Kop was bulldozed in 1994, but you'd struggle to think of another.

Benitez has finally managed to unearth sufficient evidence that his favoured Valencia tactic of one up front will work here. It raises other problems, like what happens when Fernando is injured or (more likely) Rafa wants to rotate. Crouch isn't anything like the same player, so the season-long conundrum of being forced to change style as well as personnel will (forgive me Peter) rear its ugly head again. In fact one tabloid claimed Crouch would only sign a new contract once Benitez left. Understandable perhaps, if you can believe it, but in the current climate and with the tide turning he'd have done himself a huge favour keeping that little chestnut to himself.

Sympathy for Newcastle was thin on the ground. Anyone excited by the return to management of Kevin Keegan frankly deserves all they get. It takes a unique gift to be out of your depth in the shallow end. As for Owen it was initially sad to see him so unfit and disinterested, surrounded by players clearly beneath him. Then you think back to his year-long contract negotiations and his cheap departure that weakened Benitez right out of the blocks. You think of the ten million-pound gap between what he was worth and what we received. You think of that being the difference between buying the still-infuriating Pennant or Sevilla's Alves, and then you just want him to rot – preferably in the Championship.

We spared them the humiliation that was surely coming their way and you will know already whether conserving that energy worked in our favour in Milan last night. You may even know who runs the damn club now, but I doubt it. The weekend shed no new light whilst Hicks rather laughably gave someone else lectures in business etiquette and speaking out of turn. So if Gillett manages to sell his shares we're to be run jointly by those long-standing symbols of harmony, the Americans and the Arabs? Why not sell a third share to the Israelis while you're at it, since we're aiming for peace and tranquillity? Expect more damaging leaks and internal strife if this appalling compromise goes ahead. How is any of this supposed to work? My immediate guess would be "badly", but then I think Rafa's rubbish so you can studiously ignore anything I have to say.

Until we lose again.

19th MARCH
Inter Milan 0 Liverpool 1 (11/03/08)
Liverpool 2 Reading 1 (15/03/08))

This column may be writing itself soon via predictive text. Torres...scored. Hicks and Dubai...row rumbles on. Champions League...triumph. Mascherano...outstanding again. Though all of that wasn't quite so foreseeable as Liverpool drawing an English team in the next round. Nothing was more certain.

It aggravated plenty of Reds when our Milanese conquest was greeted with far less rapture than Arsenal's. Neutrals will point to the red cards in both of our games, and that's fair enough I suppose, but the media is so damned lazy that both clubs are typecast to an absurd degree. You can already see how the quarterfinal is going to be billed: Enchantment versus Entrenchment, Art against Artex. One journalist called the first leg "smash and grab" and television coverage of the second was absurdly mean-spirited.

I was concerned for friends who went over there but there was ultimately no cause for alarm. It turned out there was even a

certain degree of 'amicaza'. A tip for United fans eager to avoid
a knife up the backside in Rome; beat Lazio in a final from 0-3
down and all your Italian travel woes will be over.

I'm sure Arsenal fans will point to the league table as a talent
gauge and use recent Anfield cup triumphs for morale suste-
nance. They would be well advised not to speak to their Chelsea
counterparts should they seek ratification for such optimism,
and not looking at last month's table (when they were way ahead
of everyone) might help too. Let's face it, we knew it would be
one of the three, and they're the least grisly outcome should we
lose. True, the manager may be a shifty weasel, his estimation of
Europe's importance entirely dependent upon how he fares in it
but Arsenal were always the lesser of the evils. Another battle
with Chelsea would be death by boredom, and the less said
about you know who the better.

This stage of Europe doesn't really bother me. Once we've got
this far we're in the hands of the Almighty and we've already
been blessed in recent years. The deity certainly screwed
around with the Inter forwards' co-ordination and accuracy last
week. Optimists cite misfortune during bad runs and pessimists
emphasise good luck during winning streaks. It's a perennial
battle of wills. This is one area where the easily unimpressed fan
holds sway. Surely a great team must overcome difficulties once
in a while? I'd fancy our chances against anyone if we got to play
with an extra man for half the allotted three hours. It was certainly more than enough to polish off the overrated Inter. Odd
things have happened in the Italian league in recent seasons,
their domination being the strangest of all.

In this and the Reading game there was complete vindication
for the Spend Big brigade. Both our account-draining buys stood
head and shoulders above everyone else, even Gerrard. Now the
opposition is about to get tougher, Javier will come more to the
fore. These are the games that Hamann excelled in and initial
doubters (yours truly at the front, choking on humble pie) must
now admit Mascherano is even better. If there were doubts over

Dietmar's role once you were chasing the game, Istanbul being the glorious exception, then Javier has shown he can turn things around.

Yes it was 'only' Reading but they put up a fair old scrap in the end. Literally. Five bookings, a ton of free kicks and the back of Torres' legs will testify to how much the referee had to blow his whistle. Coppell's cunning plan may have been to turn the game into a free-for-all once the official passed out from hyperventilation. So that's the easy run over and done with, now comes the hard part. It's unlikely we'll be this close to the top once it's all over, but should that occur many of us must reconsider our attitude towards the manager. The recent good run has replenished an already deep well of goodwill that has always been there for Rafa, and the results in the turbulent months are being studiously and craftily compared to the rest of the season.

Even without the 'Battle of Britain' – excuse me while I stifle a yawn, we're used to all this – the next two months will be vital. Thank God they are. Wouldn't it be awful if they weren't?

26th MARCH
Man U 3 Liverpool 0 (23/03/08)

Don't look back.

Did I say last week that great teams should be able to overcome difficulties? We were going to be tested sooner or later, but couldn't they have eased us in gently? A goal and a man down at the hellhole threw us in at the deep end somewhat. I also claimed that Mascherano was the man for a crisis. For sale: one crystal ball, big crack in it after being catapulted from window.

I'd spent last week reading various Red views through my fingers. Yes, we'd won a number of games and looked good in the process and I know how it feels. You get tired of being miserable. It is not the natural state of the supporter and if you can't smile after seven victories you never will again but (and there always is one) a certain temperance was necessary, a smidgen of perspective at least. The quality of opponents had to be taken into consideration, the gap between those recently vanquished and those on the horizon. Few could be warned, the optimists being rather rambunctious of late. Even the players came out with some nonsense about how United should be "worried". Yeah, Old Trafford was awash with spat-out fingernails.

I know the lad who writes a similar column for the local paper every Friday, in which he admitted he'd placed a bet on Liverpool for the title! He'd have been better off buying a paper to check the table - and a calculator. Cockiness was asking for trouble and we got it in spades on Sunday. You felt like De Niro waiting for that punch in Raging Bull. Time stopped, it took an eternity, we knew it was coming but couldn't move out of the way.

Ferguson's preposterous mind games regarding Ronaldo's safety were surely not going to influence one of our top officials. And his two-faced call for 'Respect' would surely provoke more open-mouthed astonishment than Pavarotti's speech at the Bulimia Convention. No, it worked. All week long there were demands to treat referees with dignity, but the campaign would not start with Cole or Terry or that odious potty-mouth Rooney. It would start with a foreigner playing at Old Trafford. Now hands up who didn't see that one coming? Some of the officials in England are increasingly xenophobic.

It puts us on the wrong side of the argument of course. Who doesn't cringe when these arrogant, overpaid brats rampage across the pitch pursuing their pitiful, elderly, near-blind prey? Mascherano has a tendency to over-indulge in the verbal arts, and no doubt Middlesbrough fans thought of karma as he (eventually) left the field. Yet Bennett's cowardice overrides everything. He could see Torres being hit from behind by one United player after another, and did nothing but book Torres for complaining! So much for protecting the talent. He'd already booked the Argentine for his first foul.

You know it's not your day when Wes Brown joins that huge list of awful Mancs who put the ball in our net. You thought

Forlan, Silvestre and O'Shea were bad enough, and it's only persistent injury that delays the worst-case scenario of a Neville strike. It'll happen one day. The red card took the game beyond reach, though frankly it looked ominous before that. It's harsh to say Rafa had a convenient excuse once Bennett preened and flexed, but facts have to be faced. Ronaldo is accused of not performing in big matches but in four years has now scored more goals in this fixture than the entire Liverpool playing staff i.e. one. The rebound from O'Shea in 2004 is all we have to show from eight league meetings under Benitez. It's an appalling record, one even the incompetent Souness can laugh at. United do have a better team, but they had that and more under our three previous managers and they never capitulated to Ferguson so readily and so often.

The usual Munich/Shipman filth poured out of the away end, and there seemed little reaction from the home sections. It was as if they could barely summon the enmity any more, apart from the usual snide post-match ambushes. Their revenge was sweet; an easy three points, and the harshest truth of all – they've almost stopped caring about us.

We are no longer a threat, and that hurt more than any brick or bottle.

Chapter 9

April

2nd APRIL
Liverpool 1 Everton 0 (30/03/08)

So was anyone else sent off for dissent this week? No, thought not. Once the crimson-faced outrage dissipated Javier accepted his fate and the club fined him as tardily as he left the pitch. A few fans wanted to continue the good fight, casually ignoring the fact they needed a towrope and wild horses to drag Mascherano from the scene of his barely heinous crime.

And Bennett, the man who makes a habit of sending Ronaldo off, is now unofficially in the pay of Old Trafford. Apparently. He's not a crook – he's a homer. He sent Alonso off at Arsenal once despite having his back to the incident. Last year he gave us two penalties in one game. Try and guess the venue. Ronaldo's two reds were on the road. All the hot air drew the attention away from a gap in courage and class evident when eleven white shirts were in plain sight. Our rotten record in the fixture can't be blamed on officials, and much amusement was to be had watching Liverpool fans avoid obvious conclusions.

"If we'd won those two games instead we'd only be two points behind them." Er, righto. Since we haven't beaten them in one league match under Benitez no-one was prepared to explain how this miracle was to occur. Then again eternal optimists always see a cure around the corner, keeping the Grim Reaper at arm's length. We haven't needed excuses lately, but you sense a few more may be required after the Arsenal trilogy.

Some will say the re-emergence of ownership disputes came

at an eerily inconvenient time. Even Liverpool can't be distract-
ed from the task of swatting Reading and their timorous ilk it
would seem. Now it's getting tricky again up pops the silent,
some say comatose, partner Gillett with a severe dose of verbal
diarrhoea, including that perennial press standby The Death
Threat. How long must people fall for this nonsense? Let me
explain slowly for the half-witted; the moron that TELLS you
he's going to kill you... isn't going to kill you. It serves a dual
purpose; a healthy dollop of "poor pitiful me" sympathy for you,
a guilty verdict by association for the vast majority of civilised
fans who happen to think you are a conniving, lying weasel.

How ironic that Everton were the visitors after days of
Bennett/Ferguson conspiracy theorising. Any Reds indulging in
paranoid nonsense last week should spare the blue brethren
their jabbing accusatory finger because it turns out you're no
better than they are. True, we may not have as much experience
as they do of shifting blame onto refs with bulging brown
envelopes, but only because we're higher in the pecking order
and don't have as much practise. Moyes' constant artless claims
that we were favourites for the (ahem) 'coveted' fourth spot may
have had an insidious, weakening effect on a side already over-
achieving. We should have been out of sight by half time and
could still have been in the second if we'd shown a similar commitment to attack.

The game's denouement proved trickier than it ought to have
been. Perhaps one day the manager will reflect on this season's
home draws and equalisers conceded, and come to the fairly
obvious conclusion that games need to be put out of harm's way
before possession is so senselessly squandered. The fact we
were often playing with nine men thanks to the infuriating Babel
and the effete Lucas should temper such criticism. After all, a
win is a win even if it is slightly unsatisfying. My utter contempt
for the blue half dictates all sensibilities are routinely offended
by the idea of hanging on for dear life against this embodiment
of mediocrity.

We may despise Moyes but the man's achievement borders on alchemy and you begin to wonder if he, Cahill or Arteta will stick around with such millstones round their necks. Perhaps we should keep our own counsel on such matters once we've counted the number of times Gerrard and Torres have rescued us this season. Speaking of the skipper and his torrid time from abusive Evertonians, if the manager can hear what the away end sings perhaps he should pass comment on the abominations heard in Manchester a week before if he wants to be taken seriously.

Just a thought.

9th APRIL

Arsenal 1 Liverpool 1 (02/04/08)

Arsenal 1 Liverpool 1 (05/04/08)

Here we go again, yet another column that's flying blind. I shouldn't complain of course because at least we're still in Europe. Or are we? Oh it's so confusing.

Think back to United's treble, the night the Kop celebrated Juve's goals while our team stumbled and creaked in a meaningless league game. United's comeback was ignored in stony silence and Leicester's winner greeted with disinterested shrugs. When things are that bad again we'll be entitled to moan. Off the pitch some grumbles remain. The petty behaviour of the owners continues to make us a laughing stock. It was admittedly hilarious to see Moores and Parry initially denied tickets for the first leg. They could have joined the Reds outside the away end and enjoyed the ensuing chaos.

We're gaining quite a reputation for ourselves. Eindhoven, Chelsea and especially Athens last year were blighted by a grotesque variation on the survival of the fittest. Trouble wasn't alleviated by several turnstiles being closed. An interesting idea for reducing crowd congestion outside a stadium but then I'm no expert. Even early arrivals were caught in the melee so tardiness can't be blamed. Once people were inside the game panned out as most anticipated. We've been irritated by bigoted perceptions of both sides but there was little during the 90 minutes that made neutrals lose their prejudices.

We sat back and kept it tight, Arsenal passed prettily but ineffectually. If we want everyone to give us credit for anything more than dogged resilience it might be a good idea to show something different once in a while, all "HOOF!" hypocrisy aside. Liverpudlians even moan about the critics of zonal marking! The chip presses down so heavily on the shoulder nowadays even a severe flaw in our defensive technique instigates a cacophony of squealing. Count the set-piece goals we've conceded in 2008 then talk about how we are being picked on. With a straight face, please.

Kuyt's new role got him into the six-yard box. Which is surprising since he never managed it in his so-called striker days. He later fell victim to Arsenal's virulent outbreak of Evertonitis. We can make the usual crack about Wenger's eyesight though it looked a penalty by modern standards. That's the trouble though. The touch didn't make Hleb fall to the ground so why should he be rewarded for balance problems? Because they're always given, we are told. We may be entitled to our renowned paranoia after that nonsense about Kuyt and the Dutch referee. The disappearance of van Persie made the decision easier, then? I presume we must stop gloating about Istanbul since the officials were Spanish. Some even claimed that it happening to the home side made it more obvious – an intriguing interpretation of the rules.

We've all become a little too clever for our own good. The very same cognoscenti described Cesc's ludicrous pirouette on Saturday as "stonewall", while the ten wrestling matches that go on before corners go unpunished. I despair sometimes. Back when Fabregas feigned pain at Goodison and got a fellow countryman sent off, Arteta admitted he'd have done the same himself and blamed the referee for not spotting the deception. We've come an awfully long way from the Corinthian spirit. Am I the only one sick of this garbage about how "there was contact"? Of course there was contact, it's a contact sport. Well, it used to be. The flagrant duplicity of the tumble and Arsenal's blatant desperation is academic apparently. I really should ignore the game's broadcasters and their unerring ability to inflame 'controversy' from whatever minute sparks have been conjured.

The sport really has turned sour when a full-priced so-called 'clash of the titans' is transformed into a massive inconvenience and an excuse to rest the stars. Ironically we played better with the weakened side. Until we scored the goal we needed, which naturally ended all sense of adventure, and even more predictably we conceded from a free kick. Being a first-class monger of doom I'm not as sure of fourth place as everybody else is, but if you'd offered me the point beforehand you would now be wondering where your hands were. Crouch was exceptional and if anyone has a good explanation why we won't be keeping him let's hear it.

I can't keep this up any longer – are we through to the semi finals? The suspense is killing me.

16th APRIL
Liverpool 4 Arsenal 2 (08/04/08)
Liverpool 3 Blackburn 1 (13/04/08)
We've checked the family tree of every single player and there's no trace of Swedish ancestry to be found. I only mention this in order to head off conspiracy theories about last Tuesday's referee and our sensational victory. Riise is Norwegian though so let everyone blame that if they so wish. Scandinavian Scandal, the headline could read.

Liverpool won in Europe and that generally means one thing; less than subtle disparagement of the achievement no matter how ludicrous it appears. I've rarely seen a team score four goals having been outplayed and lucky. You learn something new every week. Readers may be thinking I dug a huge hole for myself last week by dismissing Arsenal's penalty appeals and riding my rather large hobbyhorse called Simulation. One could

adopt the flustered hectoring tone of the chauvinist and embroi-
der an elaborate defence for young Ryan. Fabregas and Toure
both had a little peck at him but once again the ease with which
modern footballers tumble towards terra firma cannot be
denied. When a clearer opportunity presented itself in injury
time the pull on his jersey wasn't enough to deter him, raising
cynical eyebrows yet another millimetre.

Let us not be too caustic about our players though. If Babel's
clincher eerily echoed Michael Thomas' in 1989, Arsenal's
equaliser and would-be winner also evoked a scarring comparison with that fateful night. A minute before that goal John
Barnes had the ball by the corner flag. Rather than waste time,
as is the modern wont, he tried to beat the defender and score.
He failed, and the rest is history and a still painful memory. As
Walcott gathered speed I'm afraid my initial reaction was to
urge any player to, ahem, "take him out". I'm neither subtle nor
proud. They either resisted temptation or were incapable of
catching him once he was into his stride. It was a stunning goal;
all the more unsettling for the eternity it took for the move to
reach its dreadful conclusion.

A minute later it had been consigned to the trashcan of irrele-
vance. Whether the Gooners, whose celebrations were so cruel-
ly, hilariously cut short will let sleeping pens lie is another matter. Even 19 years hence you can set the vein in a Liverpudlian
temple a-throbbing by claiming Alan Smith did get a touch to
that cross after all. But for Hillsborough I'm sure it would still
spark massive paranoia today. Back then it seemed somewhat
trivial in the scheme of things.

Yesterday we'll have said prayers and kept silent for a minute
at 3.06, remembering all the while that it is just a game. That
ethos may be sorely tested if we get past Chelsea and meet
'them' in Moscow. The media were caught between being churlish about Rafa's irrefutable triumph and wallowing in the excel-
lence of the game itself. That's easy for us to say obviously.
Whenever Liverpool conceded four in defeat (Palace in 1990 for

example) I've been extremely reluctant to talk about the game's aesthetics.

Wenger's pain was obvious and his annoyance equally understandable, but for the ludicrous assertion after game two that Fabregas deserved a spot kick. Coming from one of the game's notorious Cyclops it embellished Red delirium in victory. That it may have set us up for more pain in a later round we can at least wait a week to discuss further. Gooner enquiries about the whereabouts of Anfield's famous atmosphere rebounded in fine style. Of course they played brilliantly in the opening segment, but games last 90 minutes.

Seasons also last till May and Rafa is now incredulously receiving plaudits for rotation since by comparison Arsenal have quietly imploded. A glance at the table might keep the pessimistic at their bilious worst (who, me?) and the difference in the crowd for European champagne or domestic dregs cannot be denied. Add Hicks' attempt to bully and bluster his way to majority rule by starting a feud with the previously despised Parry, with the manager as the unlikeliest of allies, and Sunday afternoon against Blackburn could well have been a booby trap.

Thankfully Gerrard and Torres made sure that didn't happen, even if more theatrics blotted the copybook. Yet despite the great results more intrigue and backstabbing is around the corner, of that you can be depressingly certain.

23rd APRIL
Fulham 0 Liverpool 2 (19/04/08)

So here's the story so far. Tom hates George. George hates Tom. Tom really hates Rick, but can't get rid of him until George approves (which he won't). Rafa hates all of them but he REALLY hates Rick so he'll say he likes Tom until such time as it's convenient and self-serving to say otherwise. The fans hate everyone but Rafa, and even he might not remain so favoured if it turns out he genuinely likes Tom. Meanwhile, David sits in the corner with the dunce's cap on, drying his tear-stained cheeks with the extra bank notes he got for selling to the conniving swine in the first place.

Confused? Believe me they're just getting warmed up but there's no use the likes of me getting high and mighty about such shenanigans. If it wasn't for this poisonous farce what would we be writing about?

The football? Yeah, right: Liverpool's big match was in the Champions League last night, pre-deadline, and Saturday's visit to Fulham lost all importance once Everton surrendered to Chelsea and their grumpy bloodhound boss. All Fulham meant to me was the final stop on a 92-ground tour a friend took part in to raise funds for the Ray Kennedy appeal. He was probably hoping for some much-needed sleep during the game, and he'd have got it last season. Despite a similar number of changes this time around we played a lot better and Fulham's plight got worse, proving that Rotation is only worthy of media analysis when we're losing and that Neil Warnock (whinging yet again this week) is a gigantic horse's ass.

Even had we put the 'craven' in the Cottage, as we did last season, it could not have been any more humiliating than Hicks' party political broadcast on behalf of the Hand Me Your Cash You Limey Suckers party. It says much for the putrid state of British television 'journalism' that such a ghastly, fake piece of footage qualifies as news. There he was, sat in his underground bunker watching the Reds play Blackburn at seven in the morning, souvenir mug in cloven hoof. If I were a cynical man I would say the clocks had been changed so this moronic drivel could be filmed at a more civilised hour, were it not for the yawning crushingly bored kids he'd dragged into his home movie from hell. A quip about Everton (nailed it in 3 takes, I believe) and then a cosy chat by the trust-me-I'm-plain-folks-like-you fireside. I never knew it got so cold in Texas.

Struggling to find an atom of truth through the smoke and mirrors was difficult, though it was equally hard to deny everything he said about Rick Parry was bang on the money, but once the 'reviews' were in it turns out Tom needn't have bothered. Press coverage was scathing at best, vitriolic at worst – and the fans remained defiantly unconvinced. There have been too many lies to sweep under the carpet of the good ol' boy who cried wolf. He had banked on Parry being too embarrassed to carry on the façade without realising one crucial inconvenient truth about our chief executive; you can't shame the shameless.

And what of Rafa? Many were prepared to forgive his political expediency despite their bewilderment. True, fans had marched and protested on his behalf when Hicks was desperate to offload this mouthy upstart and it seemed a shoddy way of repaying them. We've all at one time wanted to believe Rafa was acting in our best interests, and so much the better if they coincided with his own needs. He saw Parry on the ropes and tried to land the knockout blow by "demanding answers" about the meeting with Klinsmann. It would be naïve in the extreme to think he didn't already have that information at his disposal.

As I suggested last week only the ungrateful are looking at the league table and the fourth consecutive year without a meaningful title challenge. The manager is as close to deification as anyone in the game is likely to get, and if he should walk away (on water, presumably) the blame will fly in every direction but his.

It's a strange situation all right but in the Anfield hall of mirrors nothing is ever as it seems any more.

30th APRIL
Liverpool 1 Chelsea 1 (22/04/08)
Birmingham 2 Liverpool 2 (26/04/08)

The World Health Organisation lists the symptoms: boredom, drowsiness, short-term aversion to newspapers and mild nausea brought on by everybody else's hype and hysteria. Round my way they call it Chelsea Fatigue. In West London they doubtless call it something else. Tonight will be the 20th meeting in four seasons. I for one have had a gut full, as it's helped dispel the notion that the Champions League is special any more.

It was never a club I had any particular affinity or distaste for, but four years on I can't stand the sight of the rottweiller Terry, Drogba's fruitless battle with gravity and their Deputy Dawg sock-collecting 'coach'. Ah yes, those stupid white socks that could even make Mike Tyson look fruity. Another one of those minor irritants in football that somehow turns malignant and curls your fingers into a ball at the mere thought. Maybe this column would display its sweeter more forgiving nature had the Scandinavian Scud not tardily misfired in spectacular fashion. His chant needed a tweak anyhow. You rarely hear supporters asking one of their players if they're ever going to score again.

The Villa rumour hasn't gone away, and even before last week's fiasco there were plenty of volunteers to pack his bags and pay his fare. He just gets under the skin. Maybe it's the living off an old reputation. Maybe it's the red hair or the purely decorative sweatbands but with Aurelio officially the world's unluckiest footballer we can't just stash Riise in the attic before the summer car boot sale. Any desire of his to make amends was conspicuous by its absence at Birmingham and he was replaced after an hour.

Before he made his calamitous intervention, displaying all the grace of a dragonfly on fire, the semi-final couldn't have gone much better. It was a typical encounter between the two, attrition peppered with occasional skill. A word for Dirk Kuyt. All week there's been understandable sympathy for Lampard, but here's a player that's also lost a parent and never gives less than everything in a red shirt. Most supporters adhere to a strict code of glass half empty, his incredible work-rate often derided as perspiring camouflage for a dearth of talent. It is worth remembering two of our greatest 'flank' players, Kennedy and Case, began as forwards. He certainly showed great instinct when he latched onto Mascherano's 'ghost pass'. Dirk's become a key player in Europe this season, just like Garcia before him. It wouldn't surprise us to see him make the difference tonight.

Let's hope Babel doesn't start. It can't be flattering to be labelled 'Supersub' but almost every contribution so far has been via the bench and his vanity isn't the priority right now. And Torres must stand up to Terry more than he did. He should have had more protection from what was borderline bullying (Carvalho was no angel either) but once the referee turns a blind eye it's in your own hands to rectify matters. Rafa complained about time added on, proving managers find anything to blame if they put their minds to it. It was a freak goal that cost us, but not for the first time this season 1-0 was a dangerous scoreline at Anfield. Percentage football cuts both ways.

It must sound like I've accepted defeat. Four straight semi victories against one club would be unique and breaking our goal hoodoo at the Bridge seems unlikely. But think back to Anfield last season and the chronic caution that gripped Chelsea. The longer it stays deadlocked the more nervous they'll become.

Everyone knew what would happen on Saturday, even the dummies that shelled out for such a meaningless trip to the Midlands. It hasn't altered the relegation battle at all. I couldn't care less if the humdrum hacks at the bottom of the pile soil their tracksuits because Rafa selected a couple of kids. 37 other games put you in your invidious position so don't come whining to us. Everton could only have caught us if they won all their games and we lost all ours anyway. Even I'm not that pessimistic.

Let's see if Chelsea's exertions against United have taken their toll. What the future holds for our lanky second striker is another matter. He's scored in his last 3 league games with only the second string for support. All we keep hearing is how our squad doesn't match Chelsea's or United's. How you rectify that by irritating and isolating the likes of Peter Crouch God alone knows.

Chapter 10

May

7th MAY
Chelsea 3 Liverpool 2 (30/04/08)
Liverpool 1 Man City 0 (04/05/08)

It's the sort of thing a sulky child might say: "I didn't want to go to Russia anyway."

In my case it's true. I've never had the wanderlust others have. I ditched the landlocked habit of a lifetime by travelling to Turkey in 2005. True, I left my fingernails embedded in several aeroplane seats but it was totally worth it. It feels like that particular itch has been scratched. There's also unease at my fellow Reds' selective memory. As United gained experience through the Champions League, Scousers scoffed and yearned for the day when only champions qualified. A day, purely by coincidence you understand, when we were the top dogs in England with a satisfyingly smug regularity. When a gap finally appeared at the cash-trough's outer edges we buried our snouts deeper than the rest.

We do that a lot. Contempt for Chelsea's achievements has never abated despite half a decade's shameless panhandling of our own. A trip to Moscow might have been useful, if only to flush out another billionaire looking for an incredibly expensive hobby. My final plans have only been disrupted by having to press a different remote control button; it doesn't mean I don't pity the thousands who had every intention of going. Or feel for the players who would have had the chance to add an unprecedented page in an already unparalleled history. Ignore the "Ha!

Rather you than us" snickering about visas, airline extortion and roughing it in whichever tenth-rate hotel room is still available – this defeat stung like a son of a bitch.

More so since there were numerous turning points that screwed us out of victory. Riise's ghost clearance, Kalou's ghost offside, Hyypia's ghost penalty. Sorry, three years of listening to the other lot whining has clearly rubbed off. Skrtel's injury didn't help either, but even when Torres equalised it all seemed curiously half-hearted. Chelsea were rattled at that stage and starting to look tired, and yet it was almost as if they were the ones welcoming another 30 minutes. So much for rotation and a weekend's rest. Admittedly Benitez did send Pennant on as a dubious reward for turning relegation teams into fodder, but Babel might have been better since he'd already performed well in Europe.

This is the danger with being such a hands-on manager; you get blamed for absolutely everything. If Drogba did try harder because of the diving jibes it says little for his professionalism, and as for Rafa's comments about the referee's record in home games it was hard to decipher what he was implying. Not only did the mind games fail, someone told me the manager looked slightly uncomfortable in a TV interview about Torres' substitution. Apparently it isn't enough for a Liverpool manager to just lose – he must be nationally humiliated too. The goal Torres scored on Saturday got tongues wagging even more. Had he really been injured?

In the end it boiled down to this: in cup football anything can happen. We're not so schizophrenic that we can lose to Barnsley and beat Inter Milan in three days. The measure of how good you really are has always been your performance over a season. Subsequent cautious comments about next season's title 'threat' led some to think we probably won't be too close next year either and fans are naïve for expecting otherwise. After four years in charge you don't want to see a Liverpool manager trying it on so blithely with references to the seven years it took Ferguson.

Perhaps we've discovered the main reason for my Euro-scepticism. For the majority of this decade talk of a title tilt has been ingenuous and cheap. While Champions League success fills the coffers and presumably pays the Americans' loans, Shankly's "bread and butter" looks singularly unappetising in comparison.

It shows you how long it is since we've genuinely challenged that I told a friend I just wanted to take a radio to an April league game to find out how the others are faring. "You can get text updates nowadays" he remarked tartly. I could see all his sinews straining as he resisted the urge to call me granddad. City was another exercise in futility. They never threatened, even when they were losing. Since the result didn't matter in the slightest inexperienced observers might have expected both managers to loosen their shackles a tad.

The rest of us counted down the seconds till summer begins. It can't come soon enough.

14th MAY
Tottenham 0 Liverpool 2 (11/05/08)

I've got finality on the brain lately. The fanzine I've edited for nearly 20 years has come to an end, and I've got the summer to figure out what the hell I'm going to do with the rest of my days.

I'd be a liar if I claimed never to have had the urge to cut all of my ties with the game. As another fruitless league season trundles over the finishing line, the Mancs already at their celebratory party endangering the lady folk, the sense of living in a recurring dream overwhelms me. My generation saw it all. Were it not for those glory days the current generation would be revelling in these last eight years. These would be our halcyon days, not the 70's or 80's.

Welcome to the schizophrenic world of the Liverpool supporter. How many times have you been told by rivals that you were living in the past, gorging on 'historeeee'? Yet when you reel off the not insubstantial list of achievements in (please forgive me) the 'Noughties' you are made fully aware of the absence of one particular trophy and accused of settling for second best. They've got you every which way you turn, but that's okay. There are worse positions to be in.

We may be embroiled in a civil war being fought across an ocean, by clueless prospectors who can smell money a mile away but are curiously incapable of borrowing it. We may be coached by a ludicrously gifted but infuriatingly flawed manager that no sooner sees one fire extinguished before reaching instinctively for more matches. Wrapped in our European comfort blanket we are mostly oblivious to our failure. It would amaze our 2004 selves to be told of the iconic status of someone who has not dragged one title campaign into February and yet the gap has been reduced despite the extraordinary chaos behind the scenes. Let the rationalisations begin. "But for Ronaldo," we'll say. "But for Torres," they'll counter.

We seethe and simmer as the rest of football rolls over for them. Each memory oozing through the brain with acidic destructiveness. Even their enemies bend the knee; we beat Blackburn for them in 1995, in sharp contrast to Middlesbrough's pitiful surrender the following year when Newcastle wanted a favour. Leeds, of all people, beat Arsenal for them in 1999 and 2003. Now Bolton have joined Oldham in feeding the arrogance of the mongrel mill town that overshadows them. It defies logic, and the less said about Steve Bennett the better. He should be Rafa's first summer signing.

Some still want to focus on the money, without wanting to be reminded how Ferguson earned that fortune with success based initially on shrewd buys and a fruitful academy. They certainly don't want to think about Black January when we dropped those 11 crucial points to the might of City, Wigan, Boro, Villa and West Ham, nor does the one point from 24 Rafa has gleaned from clashes with United themselves particularly interest them either. Something is clearly stirring though. We've seen enough false dawns not to get too frisky about another one, but not even the gloomiest of souls can deny the fervour for Fernando Torres (witnessed once again on Sunday) is richly deserved and thrilling to one's fingertips.

I'm too old and fat for all that 'Bounce' nonsense – these days it takes at least two minutes for my body to stop wobbling – so he'll have to make do with a purr and a contented nod of approval. This is someone special hopefully without the summer dalliances with Chelsea that blocked another player's path towards true greatness and absolute worship. I can't remember the last time we put in any kind of a performance in the opening 45 minutes and White Hart Lane was no better, but if we make our move at some point in the game it's poor form to quibble about precisely when. Chants for Heskey, in a misguided belief that he'd equalised for Wigan against the Mancs, were irritating and a stark reminder that the real drama of the season was being played out on somebody else's stage.

And yet a new season awaits and a veneer of rampant idealism is already spreading like wildfire. By August it will have obliterated every negative thought in its path. That's how you keep going I suppose.

Also available from Heroes Publishing

HUNDRED WATTS
a life in music
by RON WATTS

With Foreword by former Sex Pistol
Glen Matlock

Ron Watts remains one of the most influential men in
the history of British music.
From John Lee Hooker to Johnny Rotten, Bowie to Bono,
Ron got to know and work with the biggest and the best.
From bringing Blues greats to Britain, to his central role
in the 1976 Punk Festival at London's legendary 100 Club,
he helped shape youth culture in the UK.
Hundred Watts is the informative, revealing and extremely
funny account of his days at the cutting edge
of the music business.
Price – £7.99
ISBN – 0954388445

HEROES PUBLISHING
PO Box 1703, Perry Barr, Birmingham, B42 1UZ
www.heroespublishing.com